METALHEART IS MOVEMENT

DEX BOOK

METALHEART IS MOVEMENT
by Anders F. Rönnblom and Andreas Lindholm

2002© Anders F Rönnblom and Andreas Lindholm

This book is conceived and produced by
DesignEXchange Company Limited
Nakameguro G3 Dai2 Building
2-9-35 Kamimeguro Meguro-ku
Tokyo 153-0051 Japan
Phone:+81 3 5704 7370 Fax:+81 3 57047354
e-mail:intl@dex.ne.jp url:http//www.dex.ne.jp

First published in Japan by
DesignEXchange Company Limited
Nakameguro GS Dai2 Building
2-9-35 Kamimeguro Meguro-ku
Tokyo 153-0051 Japan
Phone:+81 3 5704 7374 Fax:+81 3 5704 7354
e-mail:intl@dex.ne.jp url:http//www.dex.ne.jp

First published in English by
Harper Design International, an imprint of HarperCollins Publishers
10 East 53rd Street
New York, NY 10022-5299

ISBN 0-06-051553-8

Distributed exclusively worldwide except Japan and the United States by
HarperCollins International
10 East 53rd Street
New York, NY 10022-5299
Fax: (212) 207-7654

First Published in the United States by
Gingko Press Inc.
5768 Paradise Drive, Suite J
Corte Madera, CA
Phone: (415) 924 9615 Fax: (415) 924 9608
e-mail: books@gingkopress.com
web:www.gingkopress.com

Cover design by Andreas Lindholm
Book design by Anders F Rönnblom and Andreas Lindholm
DVD-ROM editing and production: EPS Production Limited
DVD label design by Miwa Hirose
Production supervised and conducted by Rico Komanoya

Manufactured in China by Everbest Printing Co., Ltd.
First printing, 2002

METALHEART IS MOVEMENT

Time consumes us all

Andreas Lindholm

Anders F Rönnblom

MH2

Metalheart 2
Metalheart is Movement

CHAPTER 0 [ZERO]
Introduction
Contents

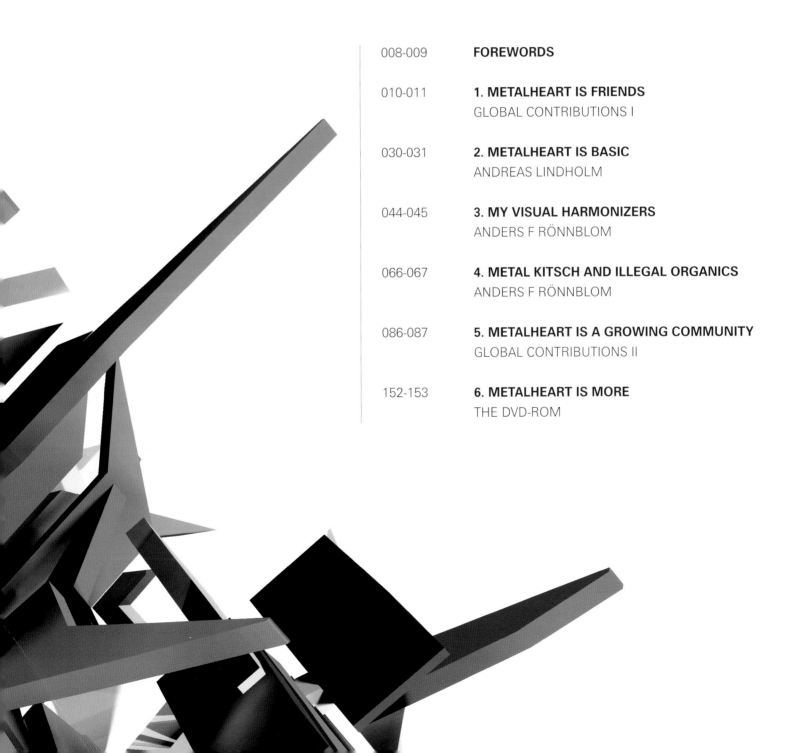

FRAMES PER SECOND

003.64   003.64

→ EXPRESSION OBSCURA

DYNAMICS_TERM

01

INPUT

OUTPUT

ANDREAS LINDHOLM

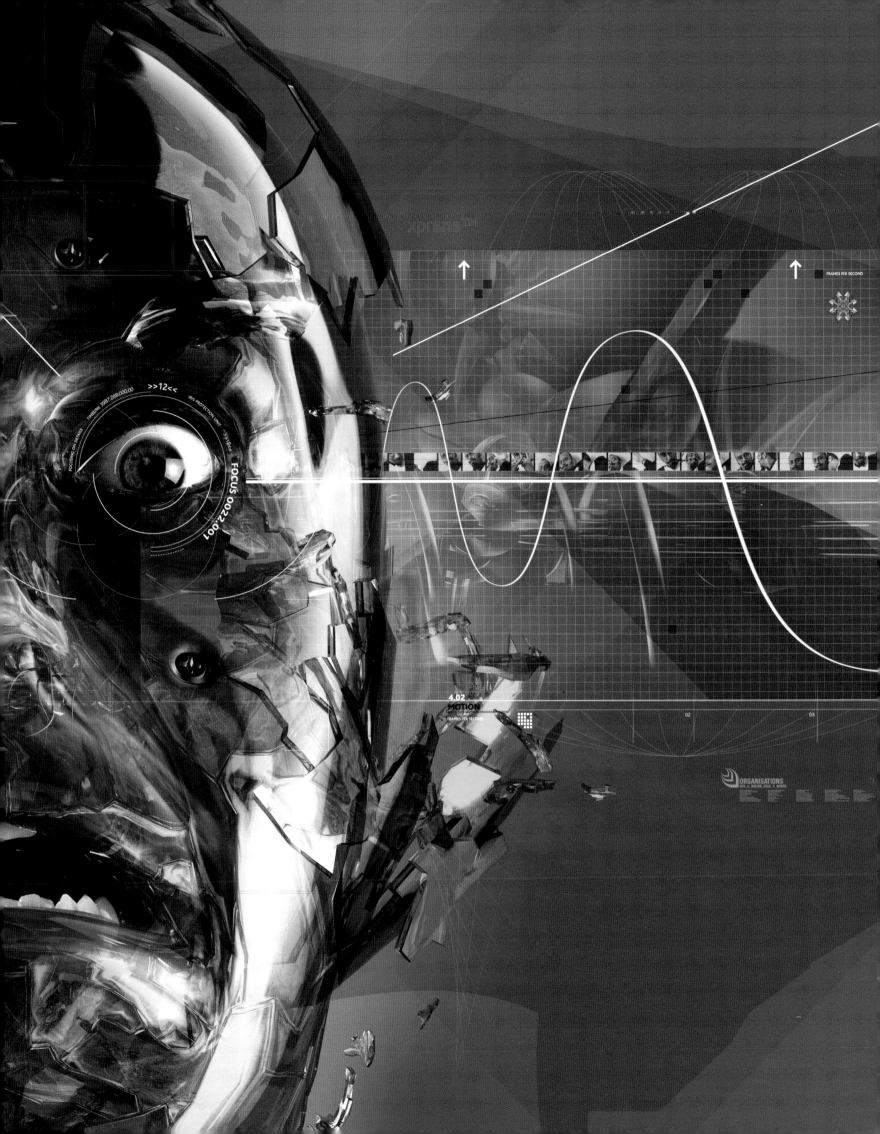

Welcome to the second Metalheart book.

The last three years, I've seen a lot of talented people coming up with stunning graphics and artworks in various themes and styles. In addition to the wide variety of graphic designers and digital artists, the new so called 'Desktop Generation' (where Desktop stands for screen resolution artworks to be used as desktop backgrounds on personal computers) has exploded into our consciousness.

There are thousands and thousands of them, inspired by all themes you can probably think of. A whole dedicated community, a bunch of individuals who love to make these artworks.

Since the first Metalheart book, my personal style has changed a little, I guess. Photoshop is no more used as my main tool. I'm a little more laidback when it comes to the expressive graphic language. I'm no longer dependent of ultrafast computers and huge built-in memory to make my artworks and design. I'm back to basics again. Starting over with a more basic style, and for me that is a new kind of computer graphics.

The 'Metalheart Is Movement' book is very much about motion. Not only motion graphics, but also motion in a more sensitive way – movement. The movement of creation and exploration. An unbelievable amount of research and computer power have filled this book with people's thoughts, emotions, ideas and innovative spirits. Sharing is the keyword for the 'movement' in the Metalheart language.

Metalheart is functional hardcore. For us, it is a way of thinking and exploring – minimalism contra maximalism.

Metalheart is not a defined concept as many other concepts. Metalheart is in constant movement, in constant progress reaching for the future.

Metalheart is frustration and satisfaction.

The rules are simple. There are no rules.

Metalheart is.

Andreas Lindholm
Co-Author, Metalheart

Metalheart 2
Metalheart is Movement

CHAPTER 0 (ZERO)
Introduction
Forewords

Thank you all for the great response to the first Metalheart book!

Like I said in the foreword of the first book... Metalheart is the description of a process, not of a result. That's why we're becoming a Metalheart community.

Metalheart is about attitudes. And a handful of other point of views that express the way we think and behave, love and hate, and generally feel and react when art and design is up for review. The Metalheart project is one side of a multi-facetted stone – a stone rich in color, exquisite in form.

Many people think they know art – they know nothing. Many people think they master design – they master nothing. What they know and master is often, a hybrid mixture of contemporary opinions of what today's art and design is all about. Some may call it trends. Some call it garbage. A lot of artists just don't care – they are simply too busy exploring new digital tools.

During the past 5-6 years of the Metalheart project, we have seen one particular graphics style that has been dominant in the new graphics language – one trend that has been exploding in print and on the web. Now it is time for many artists to set up new directions, and explore new fields.

Metalheart this time is about the power of the object, and the power of the photographic image – still images and moving images.

Metalheart is about new attitudes. And there are lots of attitudes going on out there. Nerdy tricks and undefinable design solutions circling in the minds of newborn digital gurus. People are nervous… what's right? and what's wrong?... what's hot? and what's not?

For me, this is the movement. The exciting current energy that sets the communication process in motion. Maybe we don't like everything we see. Maybe we are not into every bag of digital tricks. Maybe we just want to be niched.

Metalheart this time shows a much broader perspective. Metalheart is more than graphic design, yes! It is about vitality and openness. It is about movement.

Enjoy.

Anders F Rönnblom
Co-author, Metalheart

MH2

Metalheart 2
Metalheart is Movement

CHAPTER 1 (ONE)
Global Contributions I
Metalheart is Friends

METALHEART IS FRIENDS
Global Contributions I

Metalheart is nothing without its allies, its evangelists, its friends. Artists, animators, illustrators and motion graphic designers are all parts of this concept. There is power out there – the power of design groups and individuals who work for satisfaction. The power of creation for those who burn for their profession.

Since the Metalheart 1 book was published in September 2001, we have received a lot of contributions, and some of these artworks you will find in this book. But to be able to publish as much as possible, and keep the Metalheart community alive, we have also started the Metalheart Report in EFX Art & Design magazine. And the Metalheart Newsletter.

The Metalheart concept this time includes a wide variety of different styles – web design, photographic manipulations, fine art, architectural renderings, video clips – from students, hobbyists, to professional and renowned artists.

This time, we have several artists contributing with animations or video sequences, and they will consequently be found on the accompanying DVD-Rom. Some pieces are made entirely with the Metalheart project in mind, others are commercial jobs and assignments. We're honored and pleased to give you a new exciting collection of Metalheart art and design. Keep the Metalheart spirit alive. Enjoy.

Artists and studios included in the 'Global Contributions I' section:
Velocity Studio, Canada
D-Fuse, England
Dimitar Karanikolov, Bulgaria
Alessandro Bavari, Italy

VELOCITY STUDIO. Hailing from Canada, owner and Creative Director, Marco Di Carlo established Velocity Studio in the year 2000, specializing in a wide range of branding solutions for print, packaging and product development utilizing techniques such as digital illustration, 3D modeling, photographic manipulation, font design, motion design and art direction. When partnering with Eric Vardon in 2001, in which Eric took on the role of Media Director and web designer, he brought with him a wealth of knowledge and talent specializing in flash animation and programing for multimedia and the web. **The Horus Project**. The Horus Project is an experimental website fusing artistic digital design, flash animation and motion design outside of the commercial environment. Created and designed by the members of Velocity Studio, The Horus Project acts as an outlet for personal artistic freedom and interpretation on various themes and modes. **Name:** Marco Di Carlo/Velocity Studio. **City/Country:** London, Ontario, Canada. **E-mail:** marco@velocitystudio.com **URL:** www.velocitystudio.com

[A]

AERIALMANEUVERS
VELOCITY STUDIO

Progressions in Still Life.

www.velocitystudio.com

| the horus project_

COMPOSITION BY MARCO DICARLO
+ VELOCITYSTUDIO.COM

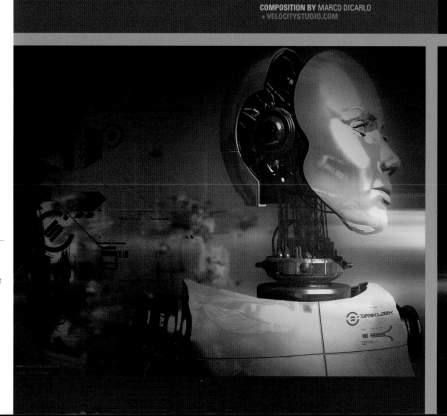

Metalheart 2
Metalheart is Movement

CHAPTER 1 (ONE)

Global Contributions I
Velocity Studio / Marco di Carlo
Canada

Page 012 - 013

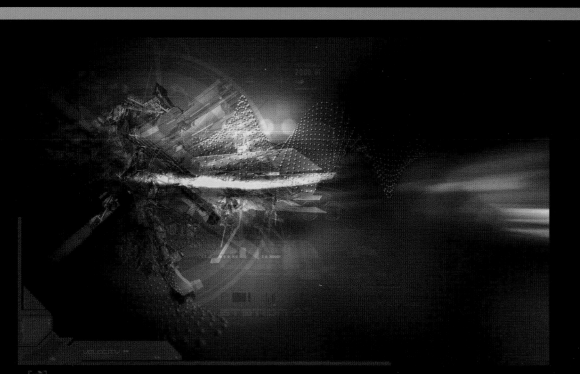

MR0&FUNCTION

velocity

VELOCITY STUDIO

D-FUSE was first conceived as an electronic showcase for new video, motion and printed graphics. They work equally in print and web design, they direct and produce music videos, and they create audio/visual installations and experiment with digital filmmaking.
Name: Mike Faulkner/D-Fuse. **City/Country:** London, United Kingdom. **E-mail:** mike@dfuse.com **URL:** www.dfuse.com

Metalheart 2
Metalheart is Movement

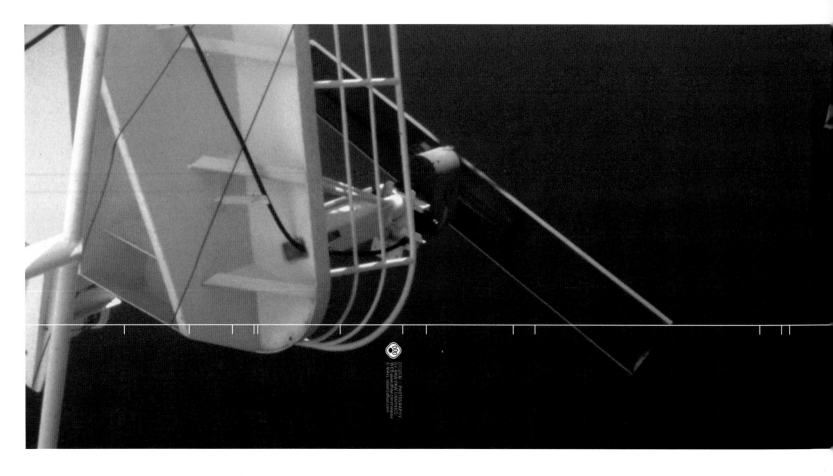

DESIGN + PHOTOGRAPHY
BY RAW PAW GRAPHICS
WEB: www.dhruv.com/rawpaw
E-MAIL: rawpaw@dhruv.com

001
002
003
004
005
006
007
008
009
010
011

GENESIS

MISSING YOU

LOVE THEME 2001

LUNAR GASES

INTERLACED EXPRESSIONS

KALEIDOSCOPIC EVENTS

SERENE

FANTASY

MUSIC COMPOSITION, INSTRUMENTATION + PROGRAMMING LARRY HEARD.

MUSIC COMPOSITION, LYRICS, VOCALS, INSTRUMENTATION + PROGRAMMING LARRY HEARD.

MUSIC COMPOSITION, INSTRUMENTATION + PROGRAMMING LARRY HEARD.

MUSIC COMPOSITION, INSTRUMENTATION + PROGRAMMING LARRY HEARD.

MUSIC COMPOSITION, INSTRUMENTATION + PROGRAMMING LARRY HEARD.

MUSIC COMPOSITION, INSTRUMENTATION + PROGRAMMING LARRY HEARD.

MUSIC COMPOSITION, INSTRUMENTATION + PROGRAMMING LARRY HEARD.

MUSIC COMPOSITION, LYRICS, VOCALS, INSTRUMENTATION + PROGRAMMING LARRY HEARD. LYRICS STANLEY JOHNSON

PUBLISHED BY ALLEVIATED MUSIC [ASCAP].

PUBLISHED BY ALLEVIATED MUSIC [ASCAP].

PUBLISHED BY ALLEVIATED MUSIC [ASCAP].

PUBLISHED BY ALLEVIATED MUSIC [ASCAP].

PUBLISHED BY ALLEVIATED MUSIC [ASCAP].

PUBLISHED BY ALLEVIATED MUSIC [ASCAP].

PUBLISHED BY ALLEVIATED MUSIC [ASCAP].

PUBLISHED BY ALLEVIATED MUSIC [ASCAP]. SEVENTH MUSIC [ASCAP].

ARRY HEARD

:NESIS

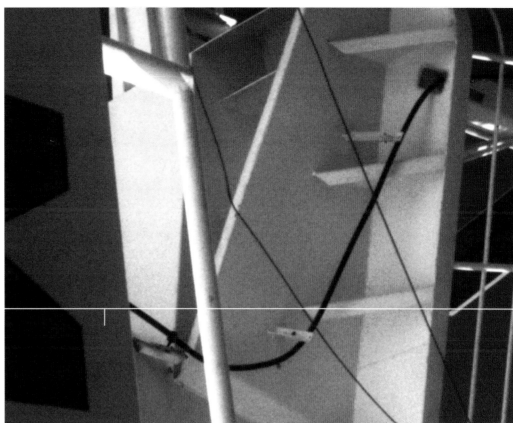

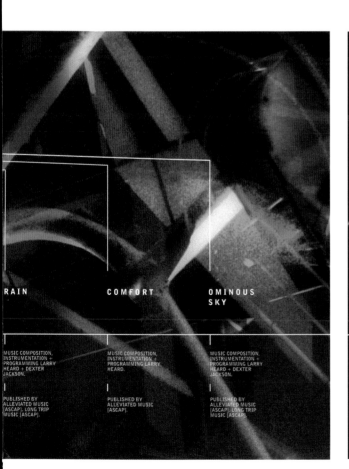

RAIN   **COMFORT**   **OMINOUS SKY**

MUSIC COMPOSITION, INSTRUMENTATION + PROGRAMMING LARRY HEARD + DEXTER JACKSON.

PUBLISHED BY ALLEVIATED MUSIC [ASCAP]. LONG TRIP MUSIC [ASCAP].

MUSIC COMPOSITION, INSTRUMENTATION + PROGRAMMING LARRY HEARD.

PUBLISHED BY ALLEVIATED MUSIC [ASCAP].

MUSIC COMPOSITION, INSTRUMENTATION + PROGRAMMING LARRY HEARD + DEXTER JACKSON.

PUBLISHED BY ALLEVIATED MUSIC [ASCAP]. LONG TRIP MUSIC [ASCAP].

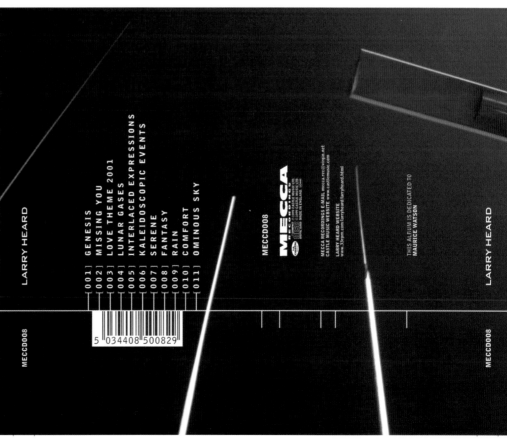

LARRY HEARD

MECCD008

[001] GENESIS
[002] MISSING YOU
[003] LOVE THEME 2001
[004] LUNAR GASES
[005] INTERLACED EXPRESSIONS
[006] KALEIDOSCOPIC EVENTS
[007] SERENE
[008] FANTASY
[009] RAIN
[010] COMFORT
[011] OMINOUS SKY

MECCA
RECORDINGS

MECCD008

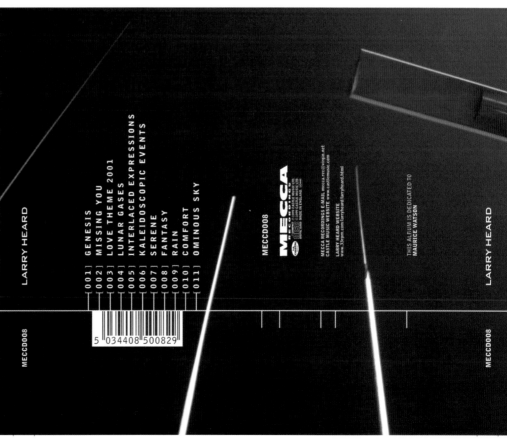

MECCA RECORDINGS E.MAIL mecca.rec@virgin.net
CASTLE MUSIC WEBSITE www.castlemusic.com

LARRY HEARD WEBSITE
www.33rpm.com/larryheard/larryheard.html

THIS ALBUM IS DEDICATED TO
MAURICE WATSON

LARRY HEARD

MECCD008

5 034408 500829

HYPERSTRUCTURE_0

4D STUDY BY DIMITAR KARANIKOLOV / WWW.MESHROOM.COM

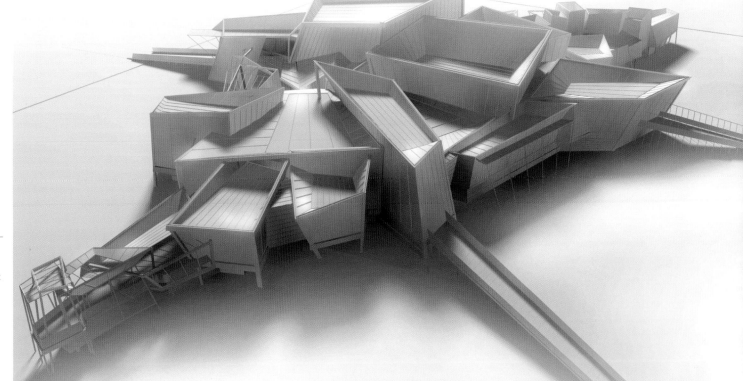

DIMITAR KARANIKOLOV is a Bulgarian architectural artist currently working on his final diploma project in the university of Sofia. The concept of the project is using of a four-dimensional (4D) mathematical model describing the "building" and it's projection onto 3D space – a process that could be visualized only as an animation. **Name:** Dimitar Karanikolov. **Occupation:** Architect/Animator/Web Designer. **City/Country:** Sofia, Bulgaria. **E-mail:** dimitar@archivibes.net **URL:** www.archivibes.net

Metalheart 2

Metalheart is Movement

CHAPTER 1 (ONE)

Global Contributions I

Dimitar Karanikolov

Bulgaria

Page 020 - 021

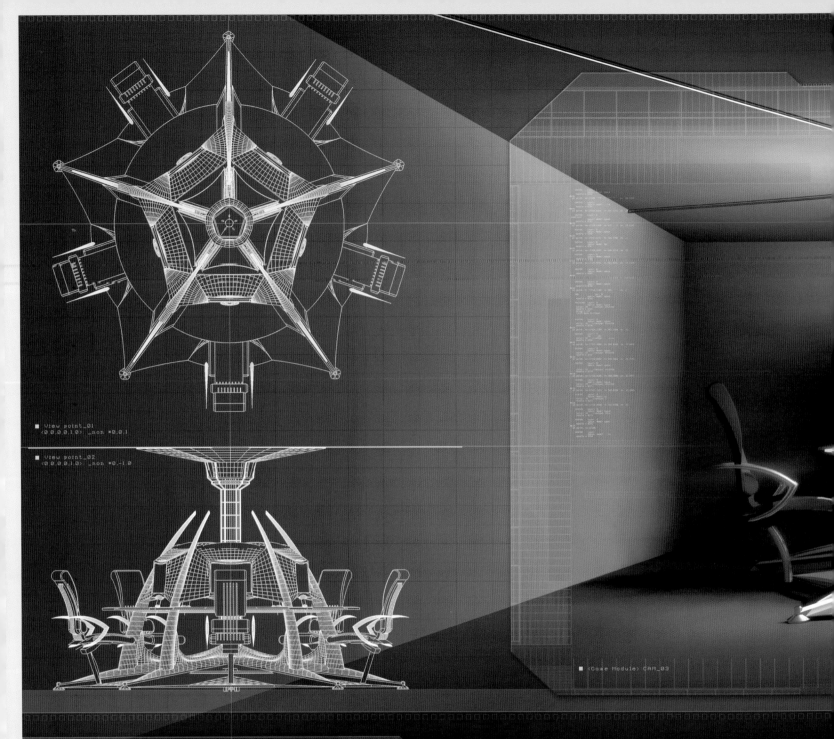

■ View point_01
<0.0.0.1.0>: _non *0.0.1

■ View point_02
<0.0.0.1.0>: _non *0.-1.0

■ <Game Module> CAM_03

NET CAFE

■ CAPTION: Study Project/Interior department/VI_term 1999/2000

■ CREDITS: Dimitar Karanikolov
■ COORDINATES: mailto:dimitar@meshroom.com http://www.meshroom.com

■ CONTENT: 1.Multiple Game module - 5 persons > F=10800mm Z=2160mm
2.Multiple Game module - 3 persons > F=6480mm K=2160mm
3.Side <Game> module - 2 persons   type (A) L=2020mm
4.Side <Game> module - 2 persons   type (B) L=2020mm
5.Relax module - 1 person L=1610mm
6.Bar module - 3 persons L=4480mm

■ CONCEPT: based on a "pseudo" WEB >>   <STRUCTURAL system>
<10 singular_point elements>   <FUNCTIONAL organizer>
<12 multi_point elements>   <VISUAL accent>
<54 linear elements>   <INSTALLATIONS scheme>
<27 polygons>   <COMMUNICATION network>
<4 vertical elements>   <LIGHT source>

■ SAMPLED: mArta/E-logic Ltd./Mental Ray console/W2K_help
■ LINKS: www.ArchiVibes.net/www.Steam.f2s.com/listen.to/yellomusic

■ L.L.Net - Master Plan

DIMITAR KARANIKOLOV

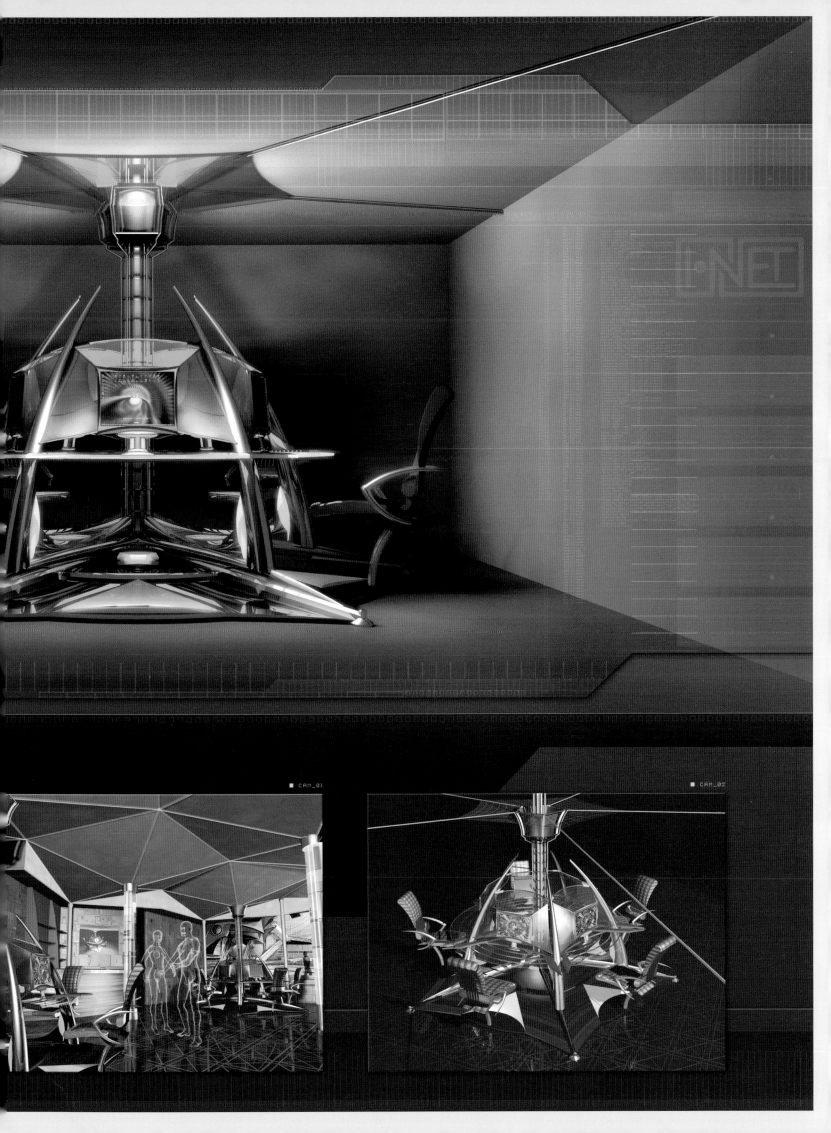

CAM_01

CAM_02

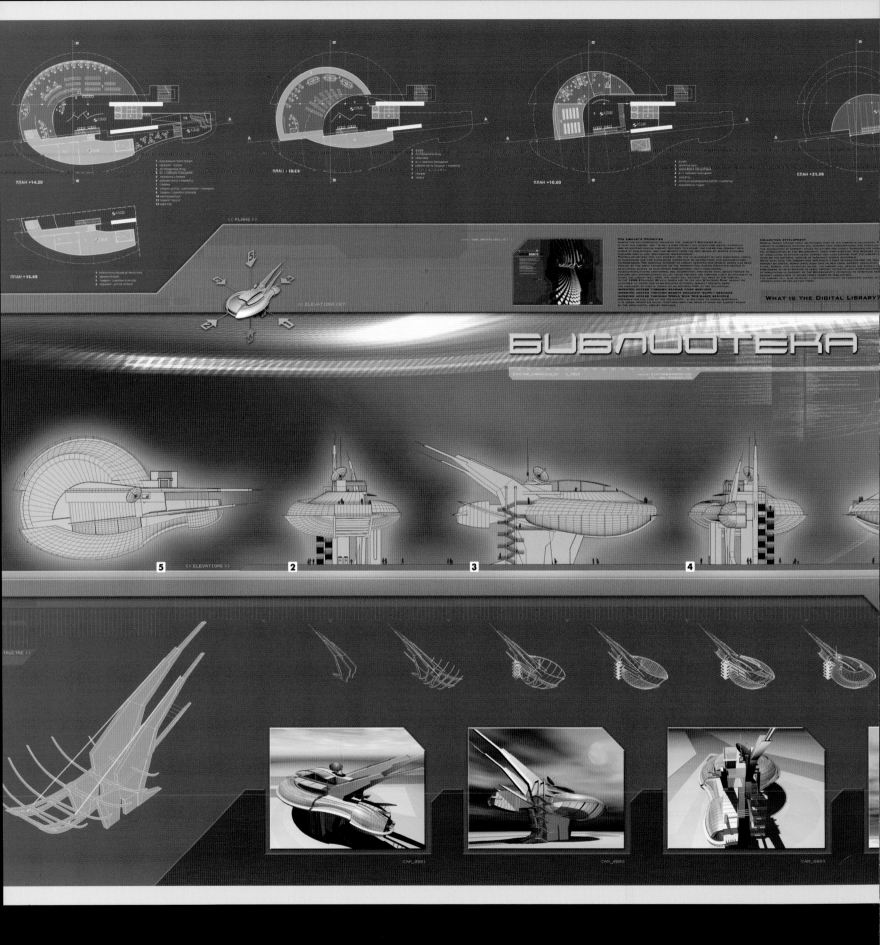

ПЛАН +14.20

ПЛАН +15.40

<< PLANS >>

ПЛАН +18.25

ПЛАН +18.60

ПЛАН +21.30

<< ELEVATIONS KEY >>

БИБЛИОТЕКА

WHAT IS THE DIGITAL LIBRARY?

5 << ELEVATIONS >> 2   3   4

<< STRUCTURE >>

DIMITAR KARANIKOLOV

B-B

A-A

ПЛАН ±0.00

DATA BASE

VARIANT 1 - 04.2000

6

LOADING

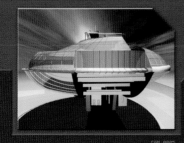

ALESSANDRO BAVARI is a renowned Italian digital artist, who has been featured in several international books and magazines. His art has been exhibited worldwide and he was honored with the Digital Hall of Fame Award 2000. He works on the PC platform with 3D Studio Max, Photoshop, After Effects and Final Cut Pro. **Name:** Alessandro Bavari. **Occupation:** Graphic Designer/Animator. **City/Country:** Latina, Italy **E-mail:** info@alessandrobavari.com **URL:** www.alessandrobavari.com

Metalheart 2
Metalheart is Movement

CHAPTER 1 (ONE)

Global Contributions I

Alessandro Bavari

Italy

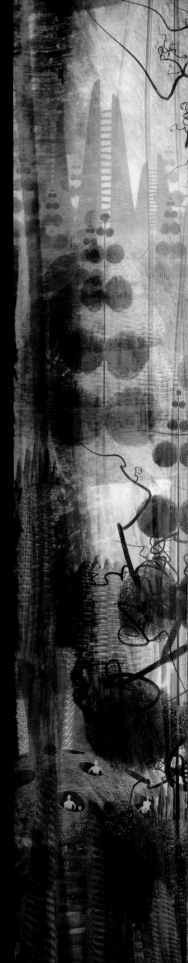

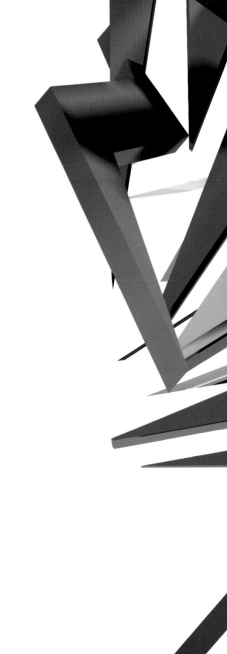

MH2

 Metalheart 2
Metalheart is Movement

CHAPTER 2 (TWO)
Metalheart is Basic
Andreas Lindholm
Sweden

METALHEART IS BASIC
By Andreas Lindholm

I'm always thinking of new ways of expressions, new styles and typography. I'm always thinking of, and planning, new routes on mother earth. I just can't stop. I'm an addict to communication arts and travelling.

For my personal interest, I'm not directly driven by making high-end graphics anymore. I've passed that stage. My pieces of artwork in this book are my own evolution in style, in pictures and art. The style becomes an experiment in itself. It's back to basics actually. Back to the roots of form and function. Back to chaos. Enjoy.

BACK TO BASICS. The pictures to the right show me and 3D animator Jens Evaldsson, Tension Graphics, exploring 'new expressions' in our seminar at the 2001 3D Festival, Copenhagen. A real 'back to basics' tour, where we played around with a video camera capturing motion graphics in realtime, by using instant lettering, dropping colors in water, and experimenting with a simple flashlight. Amusing. An alternative approach. Analogue. And easy to understand.

Metalheart 2
Metalheart is Movement

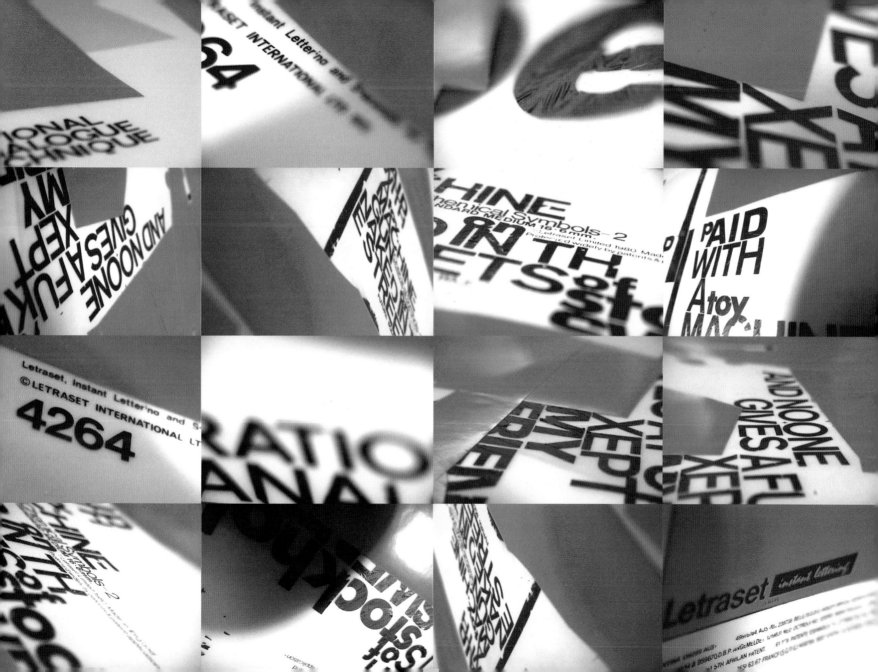

ANALOGUE TRIGGER is about photography and philosophy. The philosophic part of the chapter covers the photographic cyberspace. Where is the picture betweer the object and the film? Motion in static dynamic images. Interesting and inspiring content can be achieved in an easy way using your analogue or digital camera. Parts of my photographic exploration can be viewed here. The pictures were shot from a Swedish TV show directly from the TV screen.

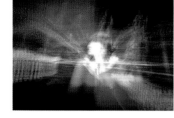
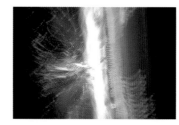

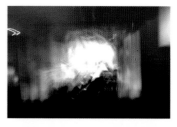
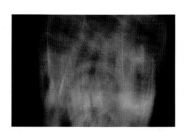

Metalheart 2
Metalheart is Movement

CHAPTER 2 (TWO)

Metalheart is Basic
Andreas Lindholm
Sweden

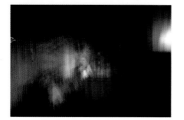

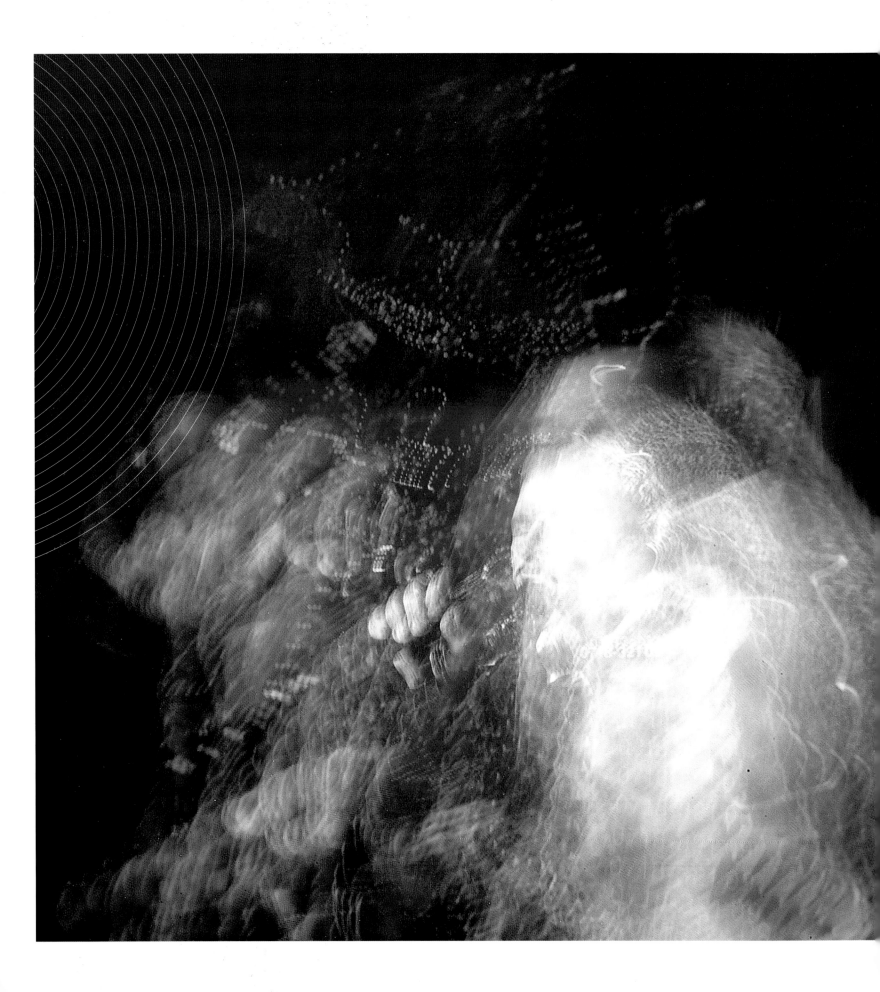

ANDREAS LINDHOLM

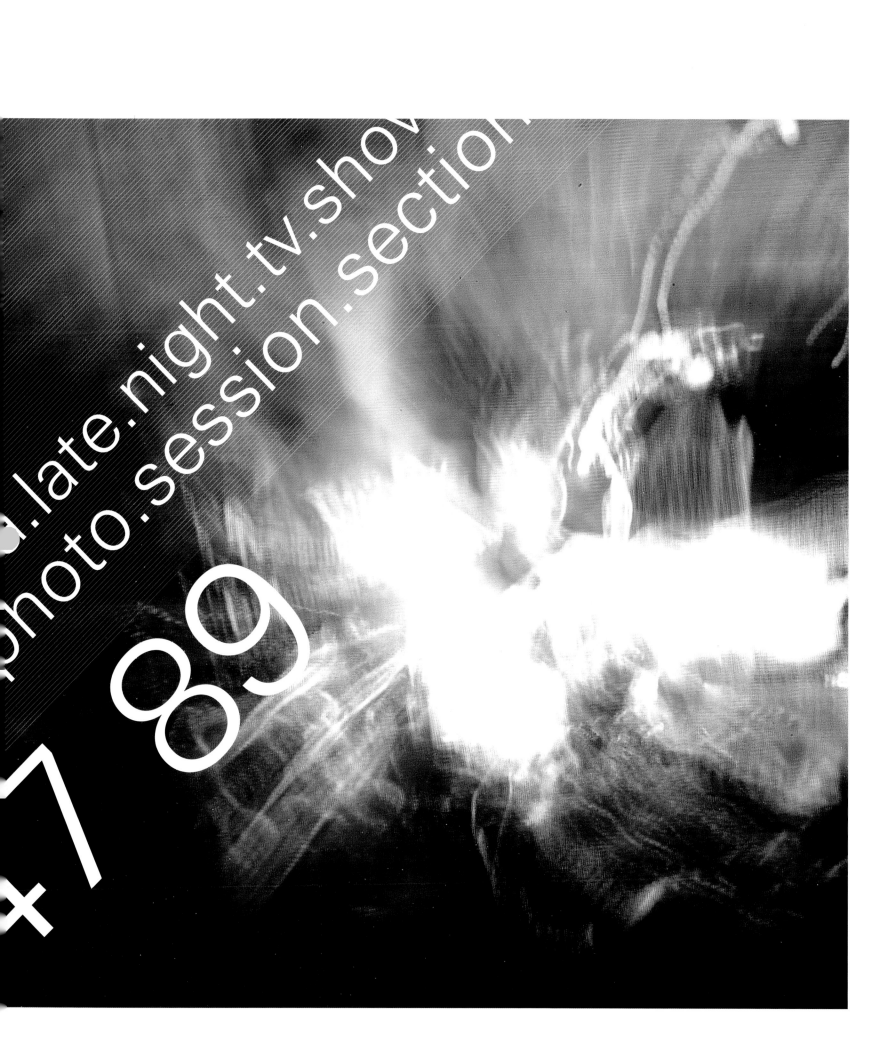

VECTOR TWEAKING. 'Motion and movement' is a static experimental Metalheart sub-project. It's not moving, but the theme is motion/movement. The following pages contain bits and pieces of commercial and non-commercial works made in 2002. The freedom of movement. The motion in FreeHand. That's vector tweaking.

Metalheart 2
Metalheart is Movement

CHAPTER 2 (TWO)

Metalheart is Basic
Andreas Lindholm
Sweden

MOVEMENT
WILL SURVIVE

MOVEMENT WILL
SURVIVE

MOVEMENT WILL SURVIVE

Metalheart where consuming many hours of rendering, sketching, layo
you can find interesting and inspiring elements for your own prog
you for purchasing Metalheart. Maybe we will produce another

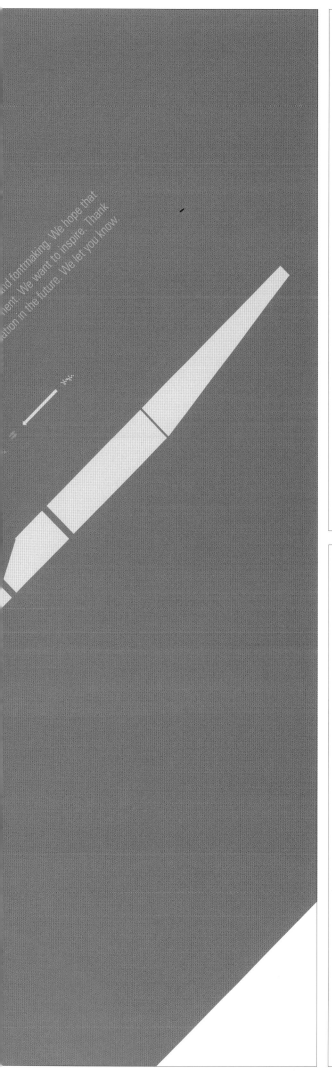

MOVEMENT

NOTHING IS WORKING OUT WELL.

It's just a brilliant opportunity to make some friendly warfare.
We want to shot you with missiles full of lemonade from heaven.
Nasty habits versus kinky shit.

TYPOGRAPHY//FUN

We all need the spirit to continue. Metalheart is a project created out
of dreams and late night worksessions. Metalheart is a refinement of
ideas and thoughts projected into this piece of print – typography and
motion parts. We wanted to do the best we possibly could when we
begun to work on the project. We where curious about our skills, how
far can we take our ideas and concepts? Can we make it beside our
regular jobs without smashing our heads in the wall too hard?

VECTOR TWEAKING. Place a curve point. Place a connector point. Repositioning points. Pulling segments. Clone paths. Push cursor. Replace interlocking shapes. Trace layers. Check Uniform lines. Create transition between two or more paths. Identify locations. Show grid. Modify paths. Snap objects. Edit snap distance. Close paths. Quit.

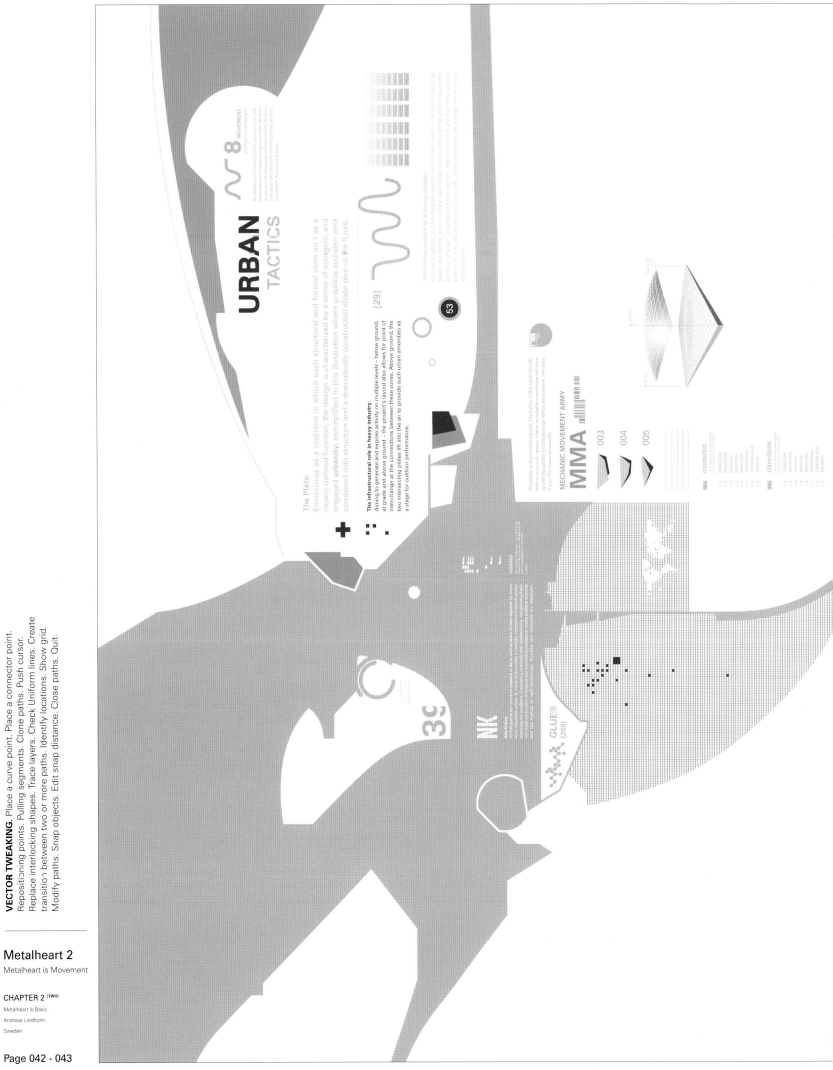

Metalheart 2
Metalheart is Movement

CHAPTER 2 (TWO)
Metalheart is Basic
Andreas Lindholm
Sweden

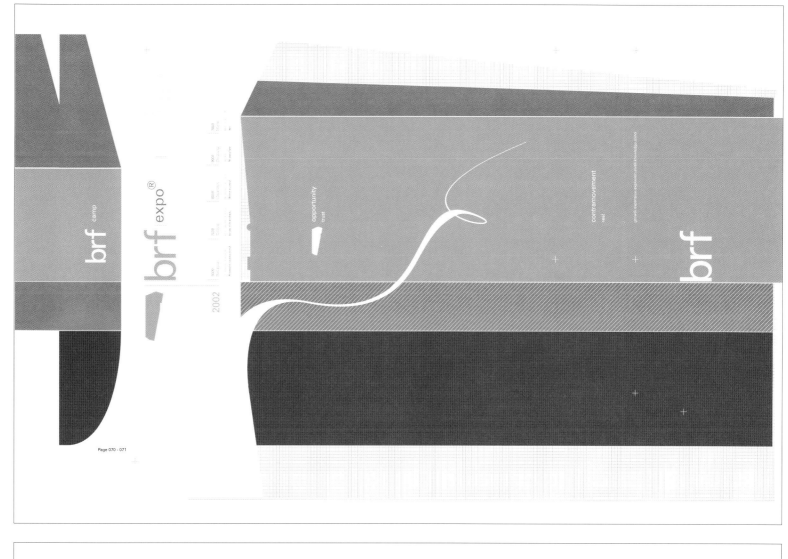

brf camp

brf expo ®

2002

opportunity
trust

contramovement
real

brf

brf

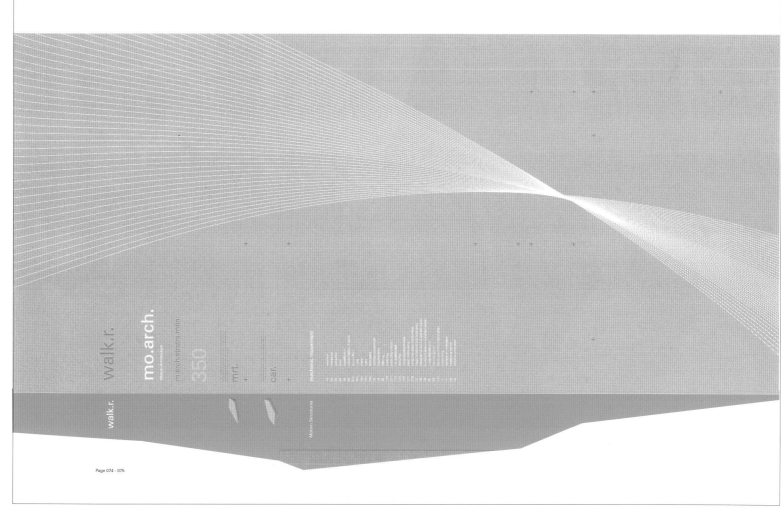

walk.r.

walk.r.

mo.arch.

350

mrt.

car.

Motion Structures

MH2

Metalheart 2
Metalheart is Movement

CHAPTER 3 (THREE)
My Visual Harmonizers
Anders F Rönnblom
Sweden

MY VISUAL HARMONIZERS
by Anders F Rönnblom

'Visual Harmonizer' is actually the name of a Delirium plugin for After Effects, developed by Chris Athanas of DigiEffects, Austin, Texas. It's a great name, and also a great plugin. Visual Harmonizer creates stunning animations based on a series of sine waves rendered as particles and lines.

The visuals in this chapter have nothing to do with the Delirium's harmonizer systems (we just respectfully borrowed the name), instead you could say the visuals are applying for a membership to the Metalheart Club for Harmonics – a harmony spot for dingbats, fonts, faces and other nice graphics. Several of the graphic elements in this chapter will be available on the accompanying Metalheart is Movement CD-Rom, for you to use as royaltyfree images.

Typefaces, graphic elements and animated sequences are created with RenderMan technology using Pixar Typestry – an old discontinued 3D type software from 1993, which is still unsurpassed when it comes to creating awesome 3D imaging.

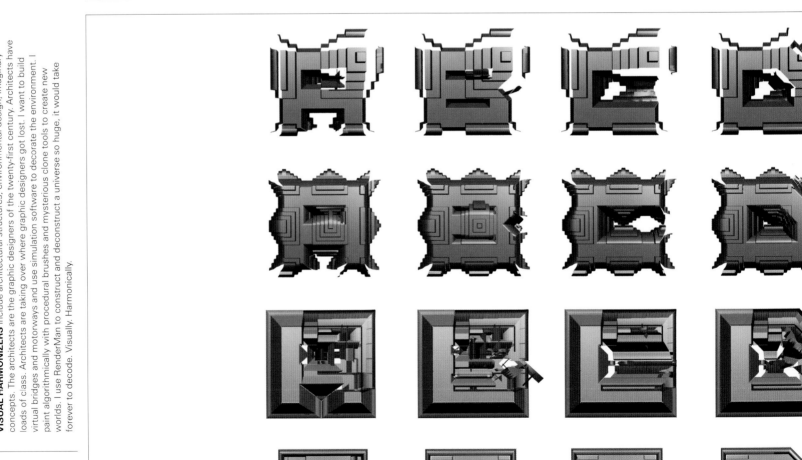

VISUAL HARMONIZERS include architectural structures, environmental design, imaginary concepts. The architects are the graphic designers of the twenty-first century. Architects have loads of class. Architects are taking over where graphic designers got lost. I want to build virtual bridges and motorways and use simulation software to decorate the environment. I paint algorithmically with procedural brushes and mysterious clone tools to create new worlds. I use RenderMan to construct and deconstruct a universe so huge, it would take forever to decode. Visually. Harmonically.

Metalheart 2
Metalheart is Movement

CHAPTER 3 (THREE)
My Visual Harmonizers
Anders F Rönnblom
Sweden

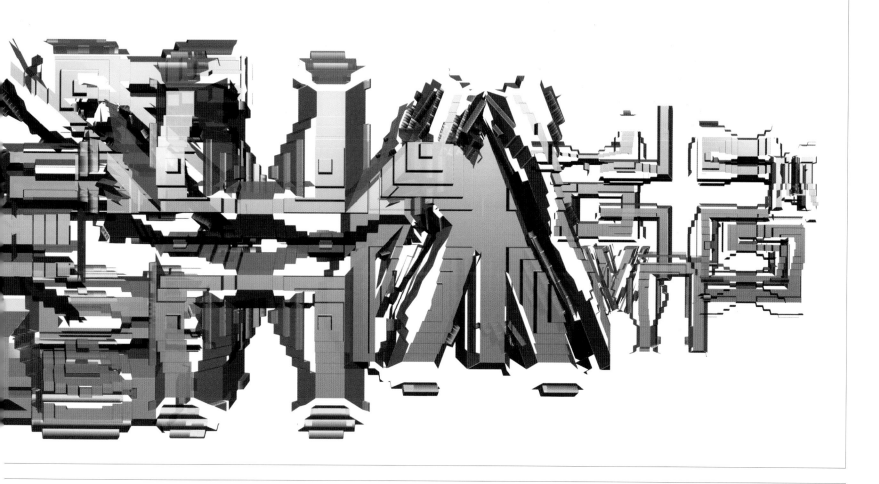

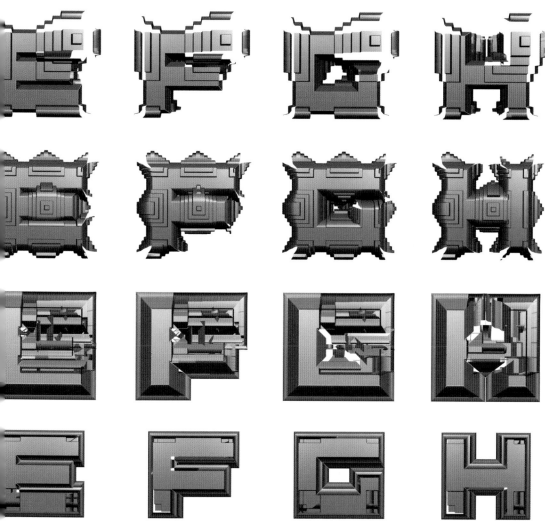

EMBOX ARCHI SURVIVAL by Anders F Rönnblom.
Based on the Brainreactor font 'Ultimate Survival' by
Andreas Lindholm.

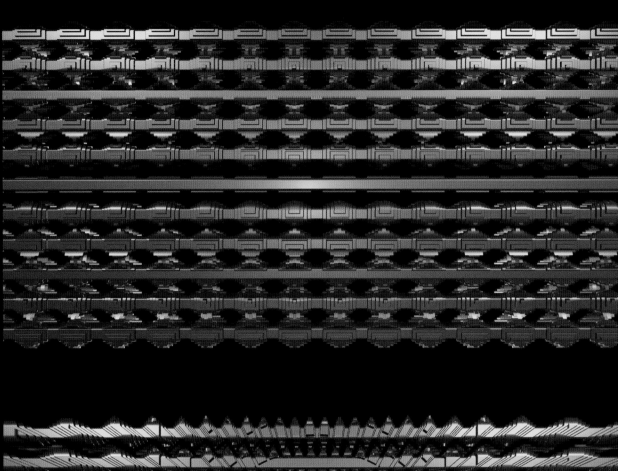

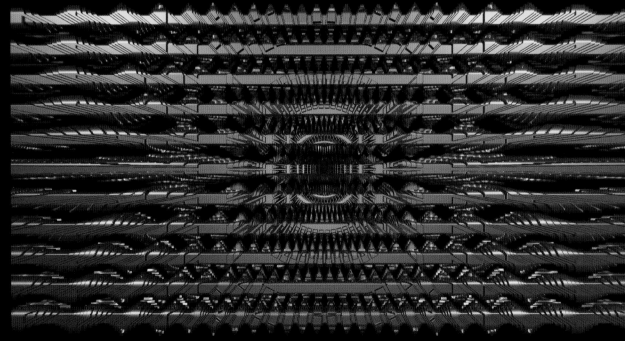

THE RENDERMAN SHADER applied to the characters is an Engraved Metal shader, a combination of a basic 'Rough Metal' material and a Barrel Relief. The relief projects the sculptured detailing typically used in barrel vaulted arches. The depth and height can be controlled – making a field of very decorative stepped pyramids.

Metalheart 2
Metalheart is Movement

CHAPTER 3 (THREE)

My Visual Harmonizers
Anders F Rönnblom
Sweden

 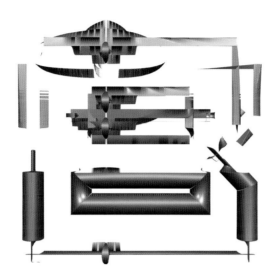 

 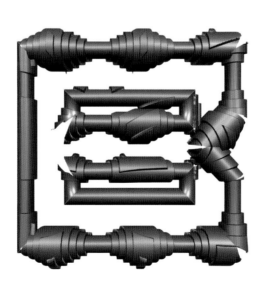 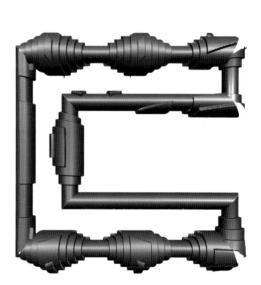

EMBOX ARCHI TUBE SURVIVAL by Anders F Rönnblom. Based on the Brainreactor font 'Ultimate Survival' by Andreas Lindholm. The Engraved Metal shader was applied with different mapping projections to characters built with a Tube method.

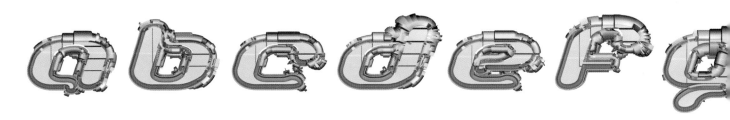

EMBOX NEW METAL PIPE by Anders F Rönnblom. Based on the Brainreactor font 'Octane Premium' by Andreas Lindholm.

EMBOX NEW METAL PELICAN POINT by Anders F Rönnblom. Based on the Brainreactor font 'Crystopia Atmosphere' by Andreas Lindholm.

EMBOX NEW METAL COUPE by Anders F Rönnblom. Based on the Brainreactor font 'Intergalactic Highway' by Andreas Lindholm.

EMBOX NEW METAL PRUDENCE by Anders F Rönnblom. Based on the Brainreactor font 'Pornomania Regular' by Andreas Lindholm.

EMBOX NEW METAL AVALONIA by Anders F Rönnblom. Based on the Brainreactor font 'Decoder' by Andreas Lindholm.

THE EMBOX TYPE LIBRARY is a huge collection of 3D rendered typefaces. The fonts used have been imported, character by character, into Pixar Typestry and rendered in Front View position in large resolutions. The different obscure surface looks are not in any way modeled, but are modified RenderMan shaders.

Metalheart 2
Metalheart is Movement

CHAPTER 3 (THREE)
My Visual Harmonizers
Anders F Rönnblom
Sweden

Page 050 - 051

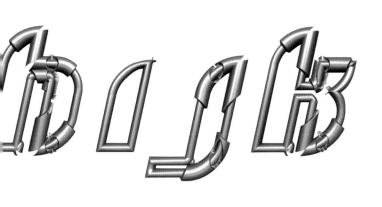

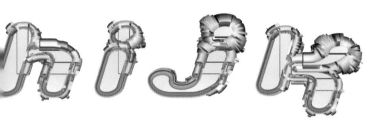

EMBOX NEW METAL QUIZ FAITH by Anders F Rönnblom.
Based on the Brainreactor font 'Industrial Faith' by Andreas Lindholm.

EMBOX NEW METAL VIRTUALITY by Anders F Rönnblom.
Based on the Brainreactor font 'Intergalactic Highway' by Andreas Lindholm.

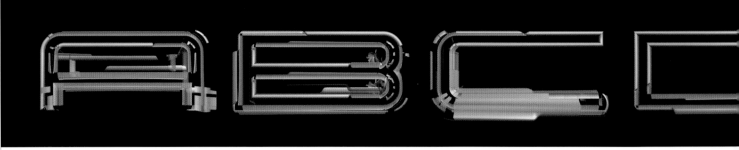

EMBOX NEW METAL NEUTRONICA 1 by Anders F Rönnblom. Based on the Brainreactor font 'Neutronica Geometric' by Andreas Lindholm.

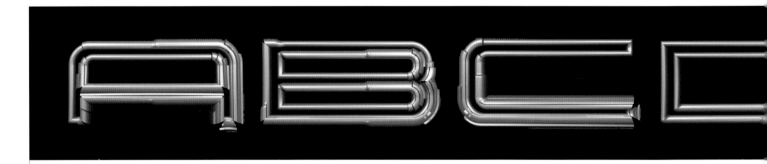

EMBOX NEW METAL NEUTRONICA 2 by Anders F Rönnblom. Based on the Brainreactor font 'Neutronica Geometric' by Andreas Lindholm.

EMBOX NEW METAL NEUTRONICA 3 by Anders F Rönnblom. Based on the Brainreactor font 'Neutronica Geometric' by Andreas Lindholm.

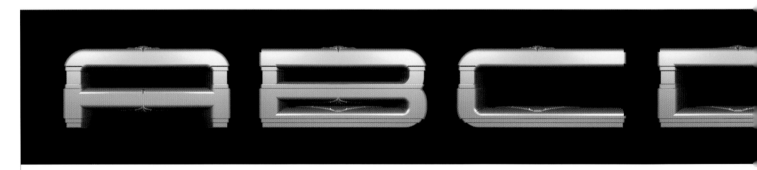

EMBOX NEW METAL NEUTRONICA 4 by Anders F Rönnblom. Based on the Brainreactor font 'Neutronica Geometric' by Andreas Lindholm.

EMBOX NEW METAL NEUTRONICA 5 by Anders F Rönnblom. Based on the Brainreactor font 'Neutronica Geometric' by Andreas Lindholm.

Metalheart 2
Metalheart is Movement

CHAPTER 3 (THREE)
My Visual Harmonizers
Anders F Rönnblom
Sweden

Page 052 - 053

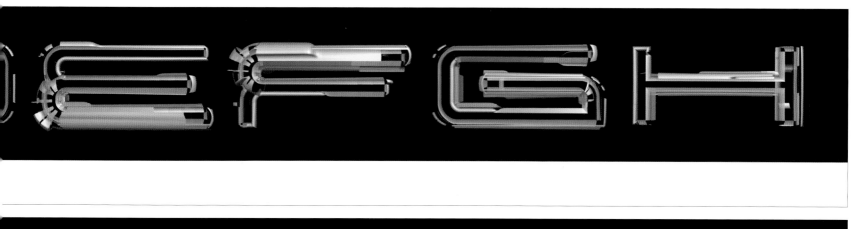

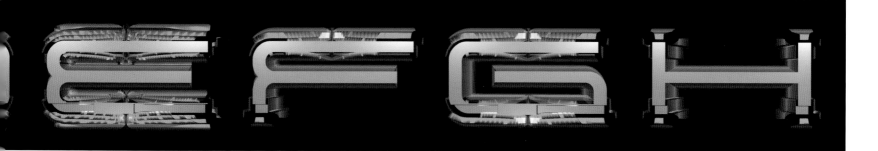

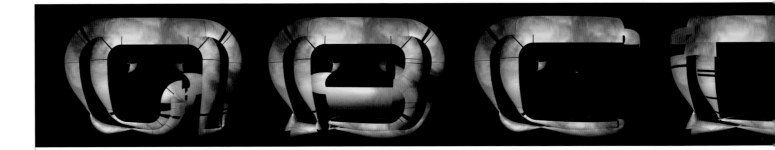

EMBOX NEW METAL INTERGALACTIC SMOKE 1 by Anders F Rönnblom. Based on the Brainreactor font 'Intergalactic Highway' by Andreas Lindholm.

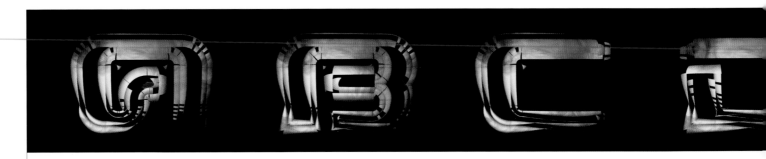

EMBOX NEW METAL INTERGALACTIC SMOKE 2 by Anders F Rönnblom. Based on the Brainreactor font 'Intergalactic Highway' by Andreas Lindholm.

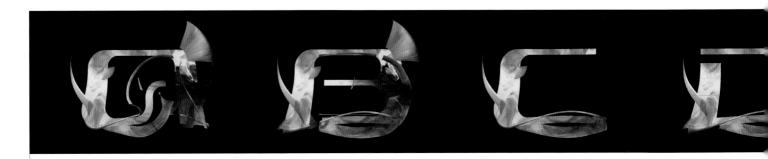

EMBOX NEW METAL INTERGALACTIC SMOKE 3 by Anders F Rönnblom. Based on the Brainreactor font 'Intergalactic Highway' by Andreas Lindholm.

EMBOX NEW METAL INTERGALACTIC SMOKE 4 by Anders F Rönnblom. Based on the Brainreactor font 'Intergalactic Highway' by Andreas Lindholm.

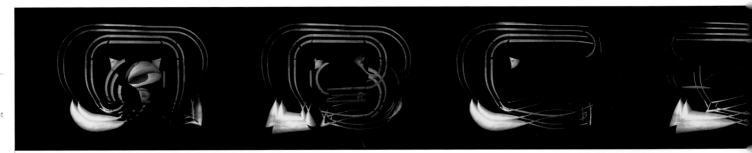

EMBOX NEW METAL INTERGALACTIC SMOKE 5 by Anders F Rönnblom. Based on the Brainreactor font 'Intergalactic Highway' by Andreas Lindholm.

Metalheart 2
Metalheart is Movement

CHAPTER 3 (THREE)
My Visual Harmonizers
Anders F Rönnblom
Sweden

Page 054 - 055

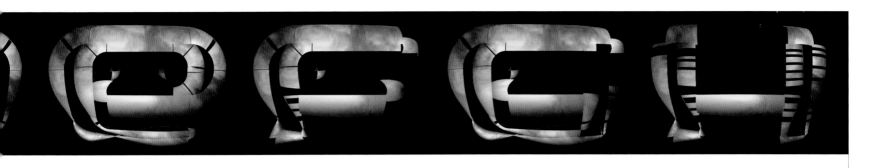
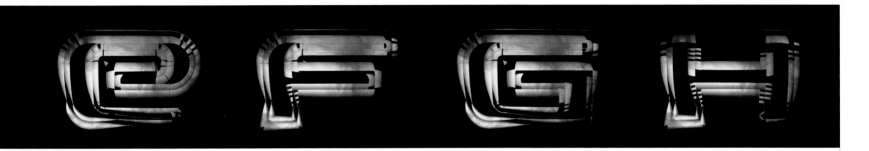
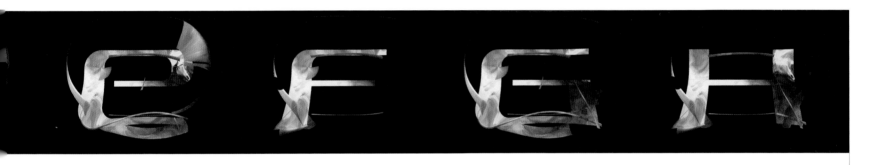
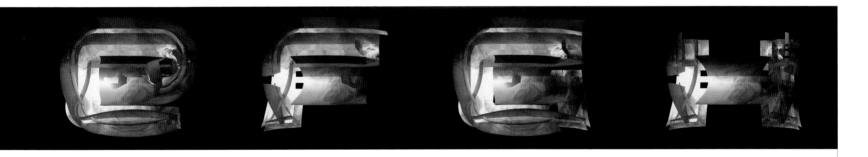

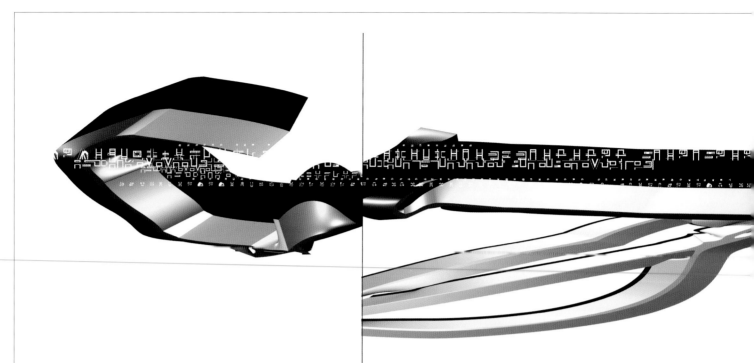

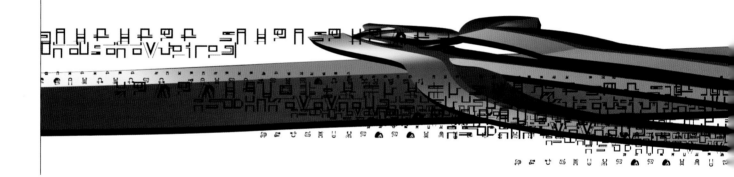

Metalheart 2
Metalheart is Movement

CHAPTER 3 (THREE)
My Visual Harmonizers
Anders F Rönnblom
Sweden

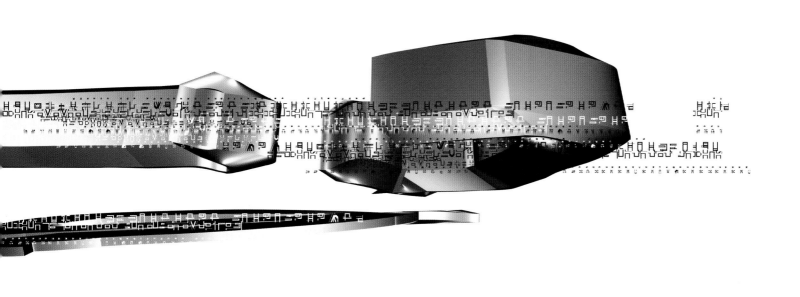

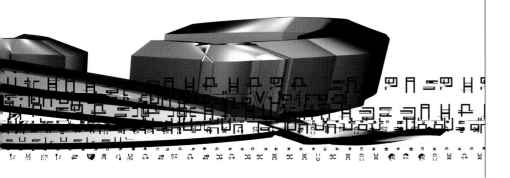

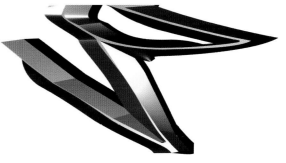

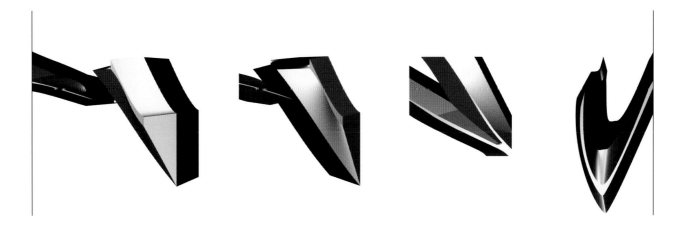

EMBOX VIRTUAL 3D GRAFFITI, rendered with RenderMan technology, is a library of more than 500 3D objects

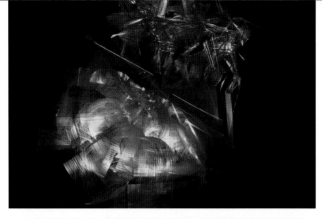

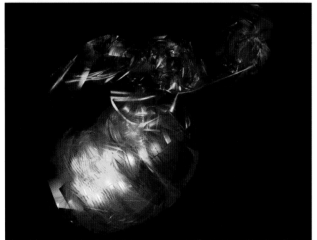

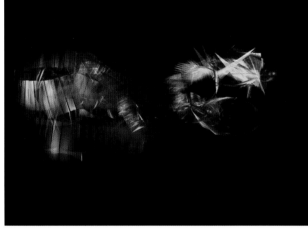

RENDERMAN GLASS. Glass sculptures are becoming an important part of my creative process, and RenderMan allows me to go berserk with glass materials. These are some of my favorite 3D renderings. The shader recipe must remain a secret, but let me tell you that it is a bumpy corroded glass that has been boosted with another relief. In other words, as Pixar used to say: "You simply bump the bumps." The result is totally crazy! Then it is a lot of tweaking with colored lights, both from the front and from the back, to get the nice color shadings.

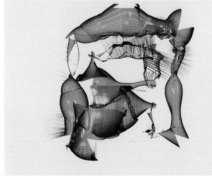

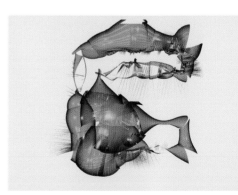

Metalheart 2
Metalheart is Movement

CHAPTER 3 (THREE)
My Visual Harmonizers
Anders F Rönnblom
Sweden

Page 058 - 059

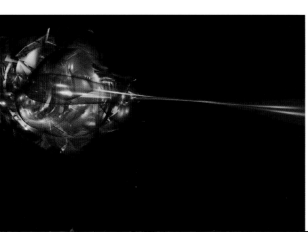

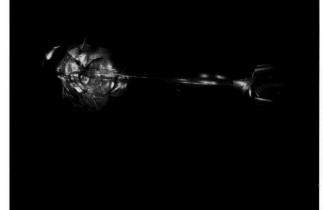

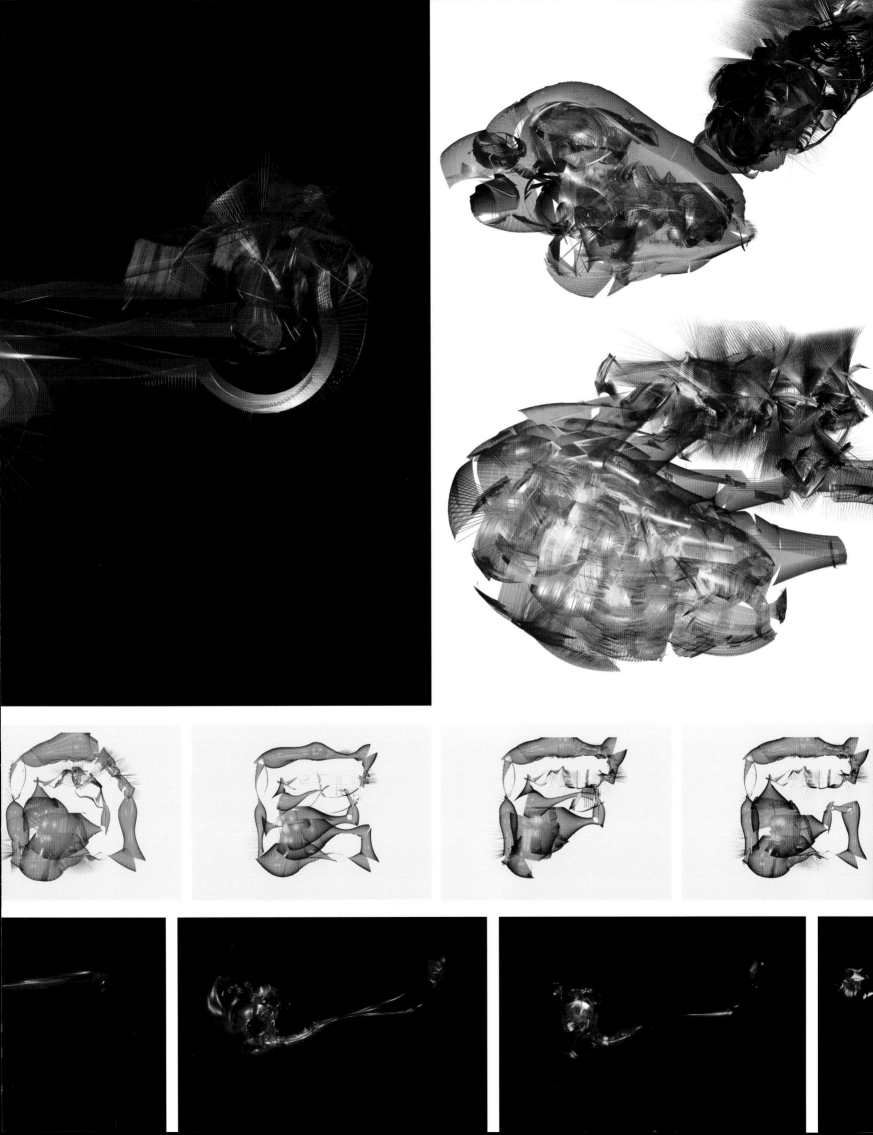

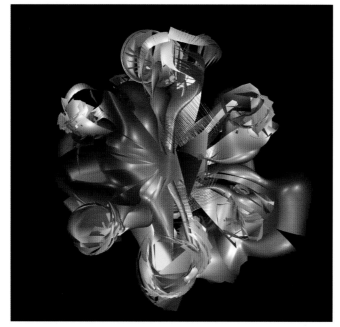

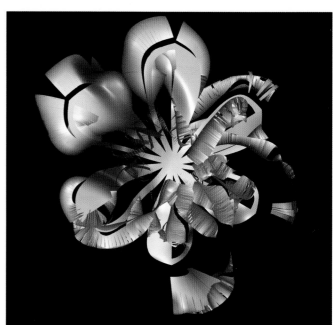

RENDERMAN DINGBATS. The natural morphing caused by the displacement shader in Pixar Typestry is a cool process. You're not allowed to animate any shader in this simple little application, so when the keyframing starts, the program automatically generates new and slightly modulated images for every frame. The displacement shader seems to have a life of its own. It's quite amazing. These images were first rendered out as still images with a resolution of 3,000 by 3,000 pixels. Then I made a variety of 2-second animations in order to examine how the displacement changed the form of the object over time.

Metalheart 2

Metalheart is Movement

CHAPTER 3 (THREE)

My Visual Harmonizers

Anders F Rönnblom

Sweden

 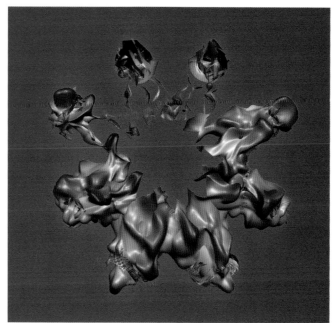

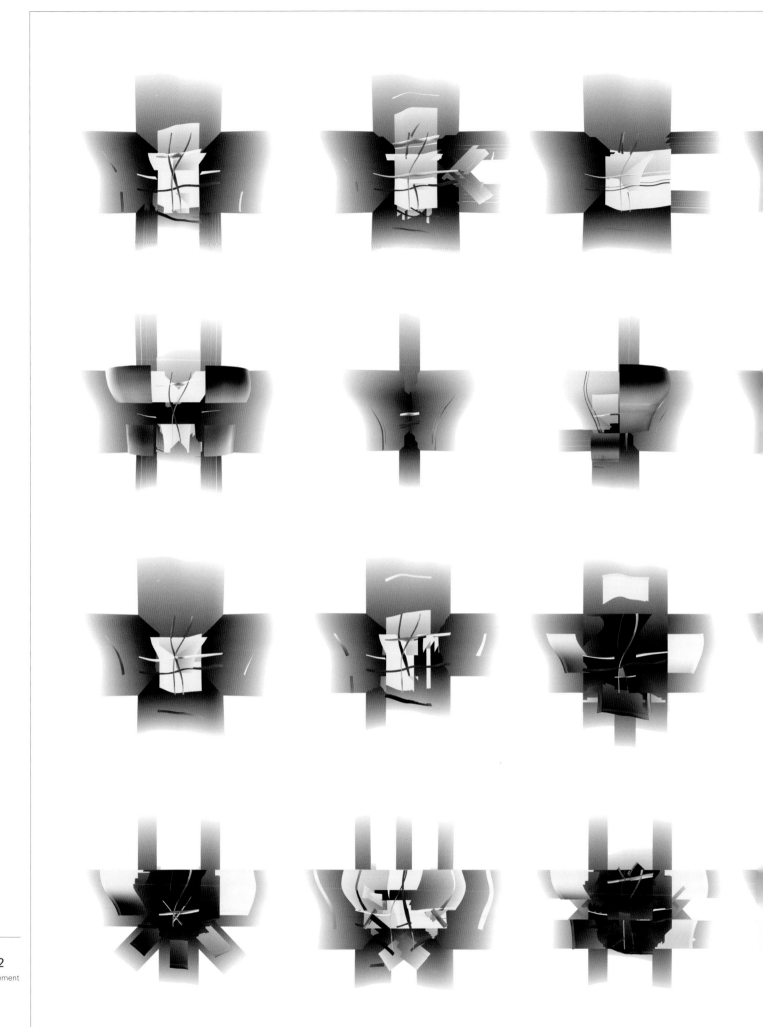

GHOST SURVIVAL. The RenderMan shader applied to the characters is a wet stone-like surface that has had its high spots worn away. Funny as it may seem, this relief is actually supposed to produce a fractal surface suitable for landscaping a terrain. It only goes to show that RenderMan can work wonders with shaders. Don't ask me how I did it, but I guess the secret here is also to find the right customized Bevel style for the character. Yes, the bevels are very important.

Metalheart 2

Metalheart is Movement

CHAPTER 3 (THREE)

My Visual Harmonizers

Anders F Rönnblom

Sweden

EMBOX NEW METAL GHOST SURVIVAL by Anders F Rönnblom.
Based on the Brainreactor font 'Ultimate Survival' by Andreas Lindholm.

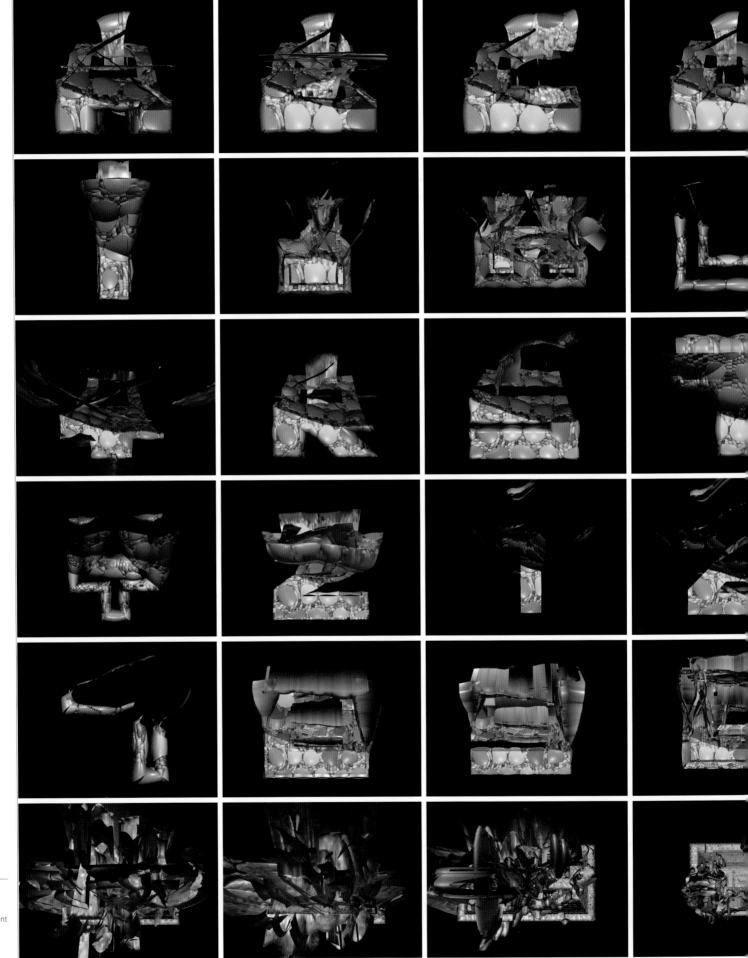

EMBOX NEW METAL LIZARD SURVIVAL by Anders F Rönnblom. Based on the Brainreactor font 'Ultimate Survival' by Andreas Lindholm. The RenderMan shader applied to the characters is a lizard skin shader and the Displacement parameters have been heavily abused, producing a wild and distorted surface, and animated sequences with remarkable morphing activities.

Metalheart 2

Metalheart is Movement

CHAPTER 3 (THREE)

My Visual Harmonizers

Anders F Rönnblom

Sweden

MH2

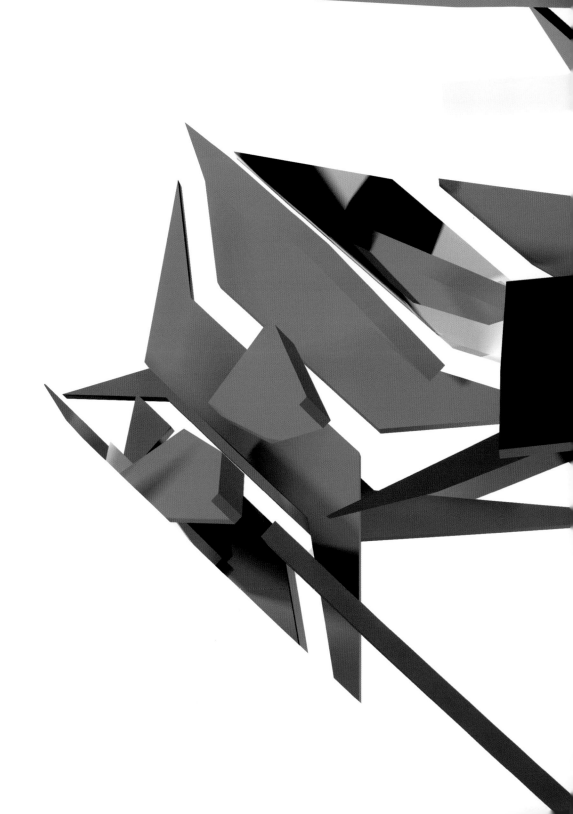

Metalheart 2
Metalheart is Movement

CHAPTER 4 (FOUR)
Metal Kitsch and Illegal Organics
Anders F Rönnblom
Sweden

METAL KITSCH AND ILLEGAL ORGANICS
By Anders F Rönnblom

Metal Kitsch and Illegal Organics is the working title
of a film project. The film is built around a huge
collection of 999 2-second animations of metal and
organic objects. The 999 animated sequences will be
used in different ways in the movie – they will be
designed as loops and used 'as is', and also merged
and composited with each other or with conventional
video footage.

Lateral thinking later gave me the 'Metal Kitsch
Overdose' and the 'Interbrain Appendix' concepts –
two more Metalheart collections of royaltyfree media
published by Agosto Inc. in Tokyo.

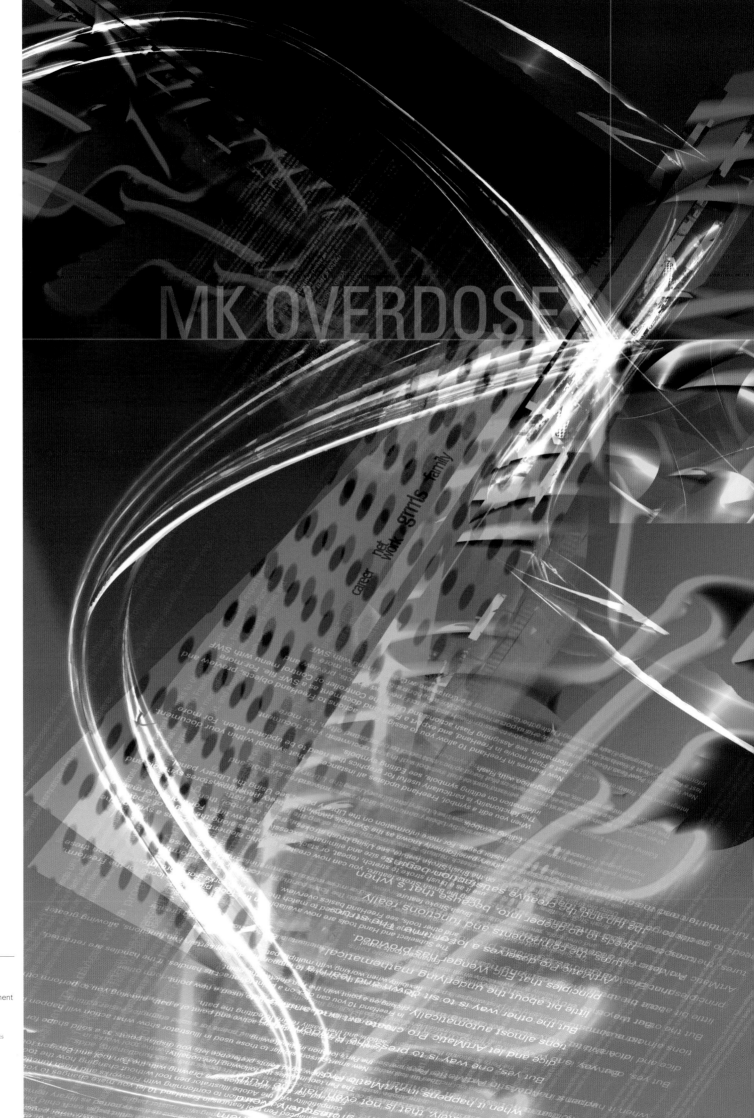

MK OVERDOSE

METAL KITSCH OVERDOSE. Metalheart emotions. Objects created with RenderMan technology. At first, 100 objects were created using Illustrator paths manipulated with KPT VectorEffects. These were loaded into Pixar Typestry and processed with the Tube method. This was just the beginning. Everything was so smooth. The material is a smooth metal with amorphous simulated reflections. This material will work best on objects with lots of curved surfaces. The process of creating these elements were repeated over and over again with various extrusion settings. I never achieved this kind of smoothness in any other 3D application. I love this. This, for me, is Metalheart emotions.

Metalheart 2
Metalheart is Movement

me
naker   knowledge

CHECKLIST 10: LAYING OUT AND P...   ...AS A HEADING... random selection
...produce a number of... • Produce these
...letters • Vary the thickness and density of
exemfidraught(7.6%)

CHECKLIST 11: CHAN...   ...THE HEADINGS • Establish... reduce your
forms • Cha...   ...of letters • Move these around... close... area •
...in the...   ...Use different instruments.

CHECKLIST 35: MIXING HEADINGS AND
TEXT AROUND FREE SHAPES
• Make some geometric shapes with your tex...
• Apply your shapes to cut into your text.
• Try different weights of text.
• Try different emphasis of shap...
• Try different proportion... text.
• Try different proportion...
• Decide on the m...

CHECKLIST 34: BRI... PLS AND ILLUSTRATIONS TOGETHER
...
...

CHECKLIST 13: INTRODUCING
HEADINGS AND LINES OF TEXT TO
VARIOUS SHAP... • Draw up a number of design areas. • Produce a number of... • Decide on the form and
position of your main address in
your text as a series of...
number of...
balance...

ANDERS F RÖNNBLOM

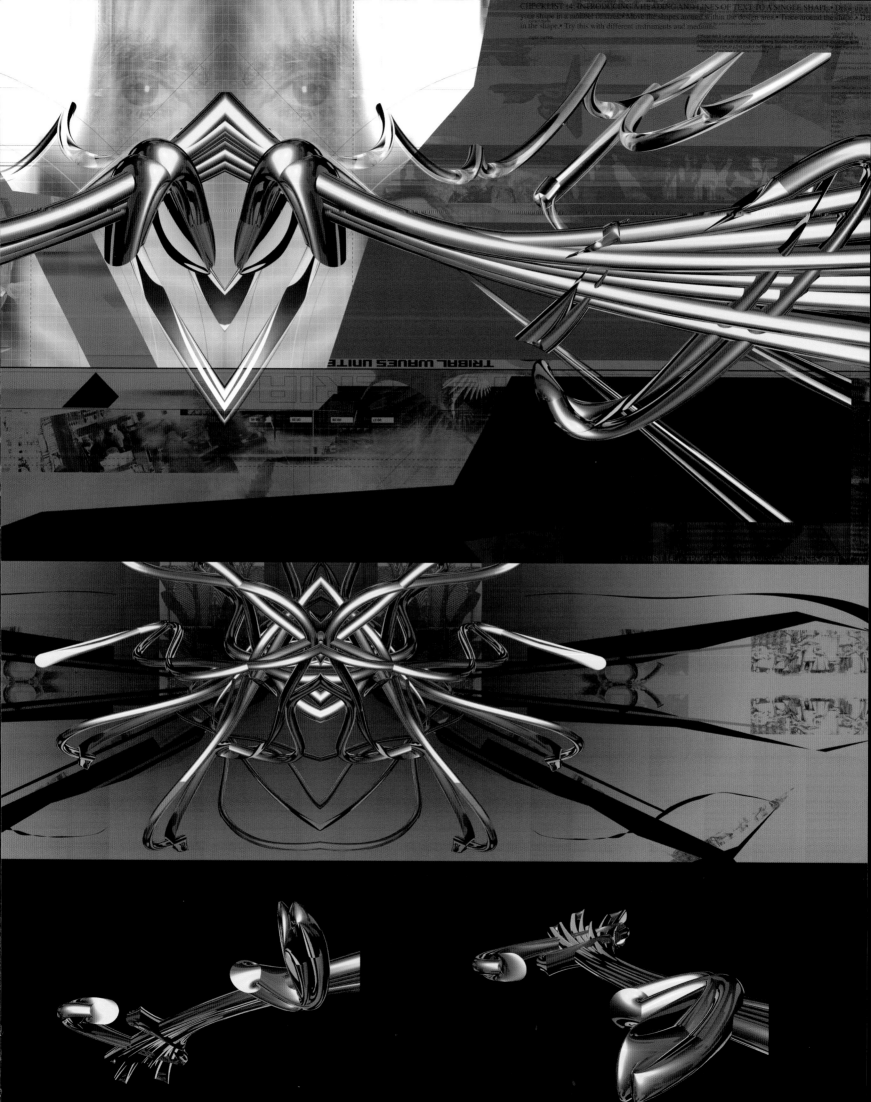

CHECKLIST 14: INTRODUCING A HEADING AND LINES OF TEXT TO A SINGLE SHAPE • Draw up
your shape in a number of sizes • Move the shapes around within the design area • Trace around the shape • D
in the shape • Try this with different instruments and mediums.

TRIBAL WAVES UNITE

INTERBRAIN APPENDIX. Organic objects with extreme distorted shaders. I wanted to redefine my values. Loops. Yes, at one time I only wanted to create loops. I guess it can also be called patterns. Like hybrid mixtures of automation – morphing and blending. It's sometimes metal and sometimes something very soft. Too much of it – and it will kill you. These loops went from being straight and smooth, to becoming more and more cut-up and corrupted. Still very appealing though. I worked them over with my lateral strategies – elemental projections, mutating fragments into oblivion. And all I wanted to see was something that could be characterized as idiosyncratic loops and derivative visuals.

Metalheart 2

Metalheart is Movement

CHAPTER 4 (FOUR)

Metal Kitsch and Illegal Organics

Anders F Rönnblom

Sweden

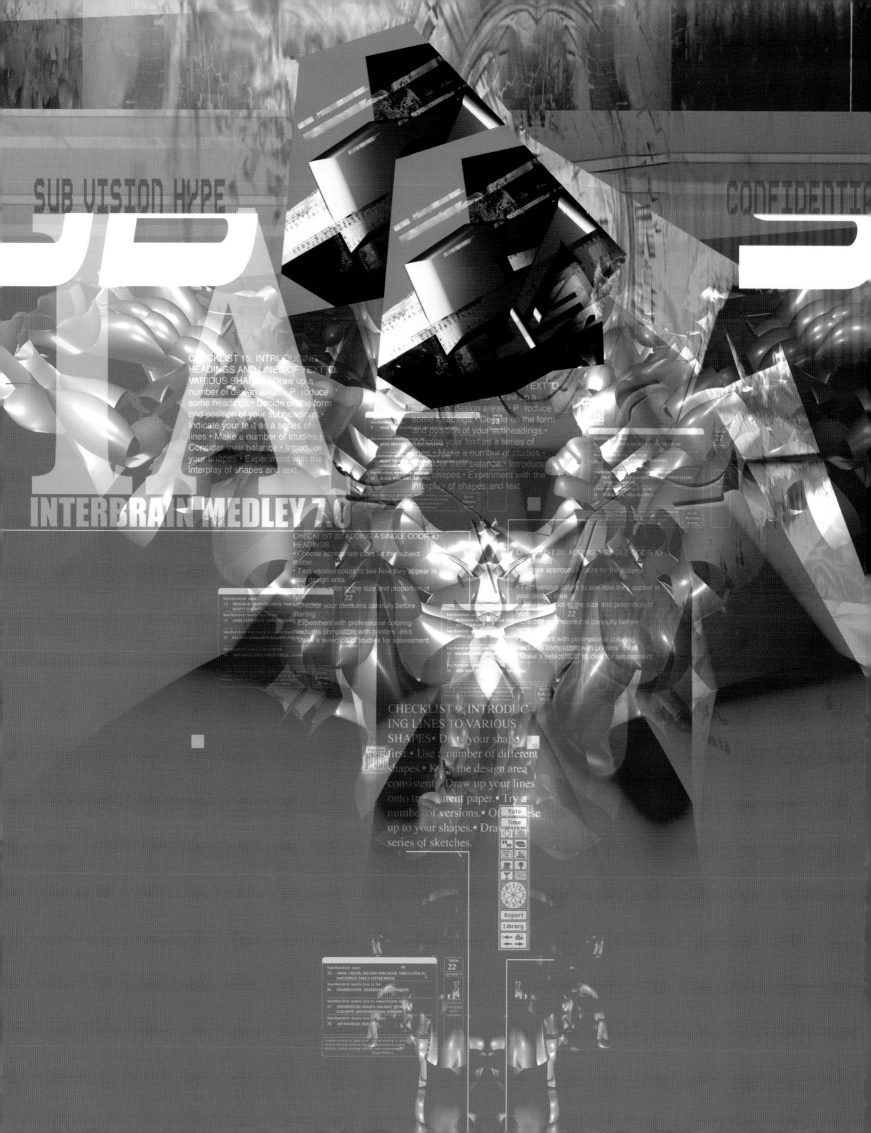

CHECKLIST 15: INTRODUCING
HEADINGS AND LINES OF TEXT TO
VARIOUS SHAPES • Draw up a
number of design areas. • Produce
some headings. • Decide on the form
and position of your subheadings. •
Indicate your text as a series of
lines. • Make a number of studies. •
Consider their balance. • Introduce
your shapes. • Experiment with the
interplay of shapes and text.

INTERBRAIN MEDLEY 7.0

CHECKLIST 20: ADDING A SINGLE COLOR TO
HEADINGS
• Choose appropriate colors for the subject
matter.
• Test various colors to see how they appear in
your design area.
• Relate color to the size and proportion of
type.
• Choose your mediums carefully before
starting.
• Experiment with professional coloring
mediums compatible with printers' inks.
• Make a selection of studies for assessment.

CHECKLIST 9: INTRODUC
ING LINES TO VARIOUS
SHAPES • Draw your shape
first. • Use a number of different
shapes. • Keep the design area
consistent. • Draw up your lines
onto transparent paper. • Try a
number of versions. • Often these
up to your shapes. • Draw a
series of sketches.

ANDERS F RÖNNBLOM

Metalheart 2

Metalheart is Movement

Metal Kitsch and Illegal Organics

Anders F Rönnblom

Sweden

IT'S ONLY SHADERS – AND I LIKE IT. Once again, the 100 objects that were created using Illustrator paths manipulated with KPT VectorEffects, were loaded into Pixar Typestry and processed with the Tube method. The Displacement parameter was heavily abused, and organic forms just exploded. No models – just RenderMan shaders.

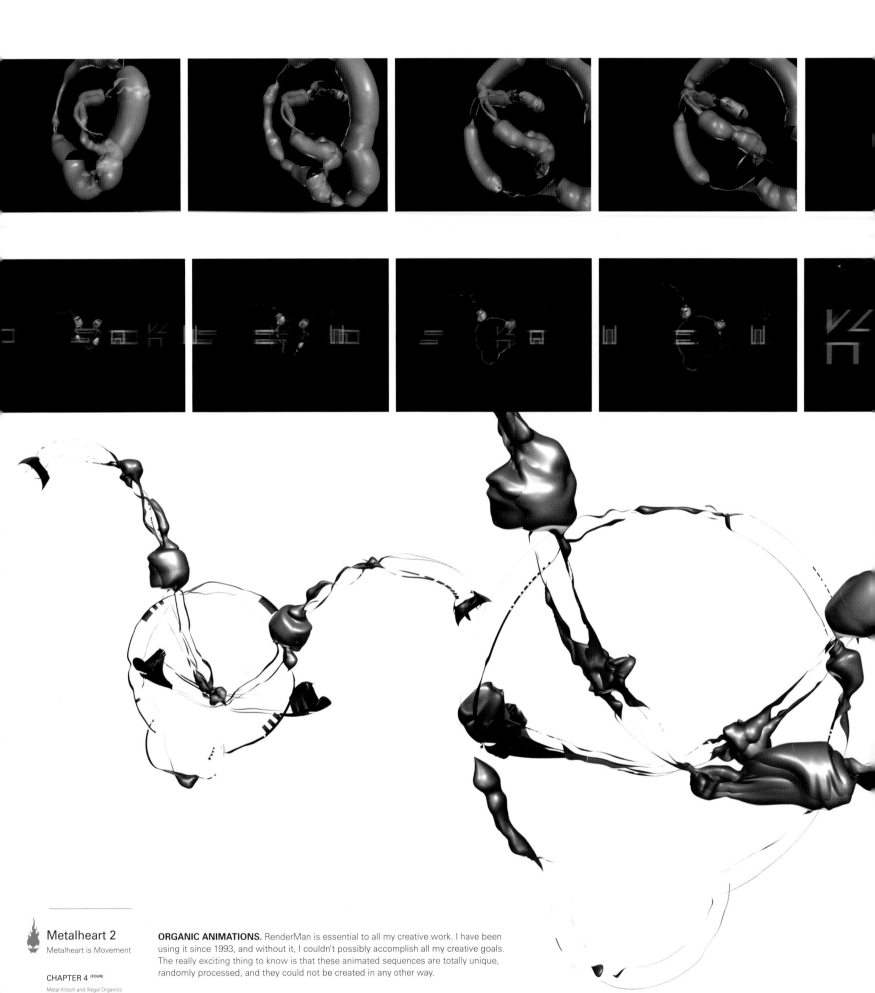

Metalheart 2

Metalheart is Movement

CHAPTER 4 (FOUR)

Metal Kitsch and Illegal Organics

Anders F Rönnblom

Sweden

ORGANIC ANIMATIONS. RenderMan is essential to all my creative work. I have been using it since 1993, and without it, I couldn't possibly accomplish all my creative goals. The really exciting thing to know is that these animated sequences are totally unique, randomly processed, and they could not be created in any other way.

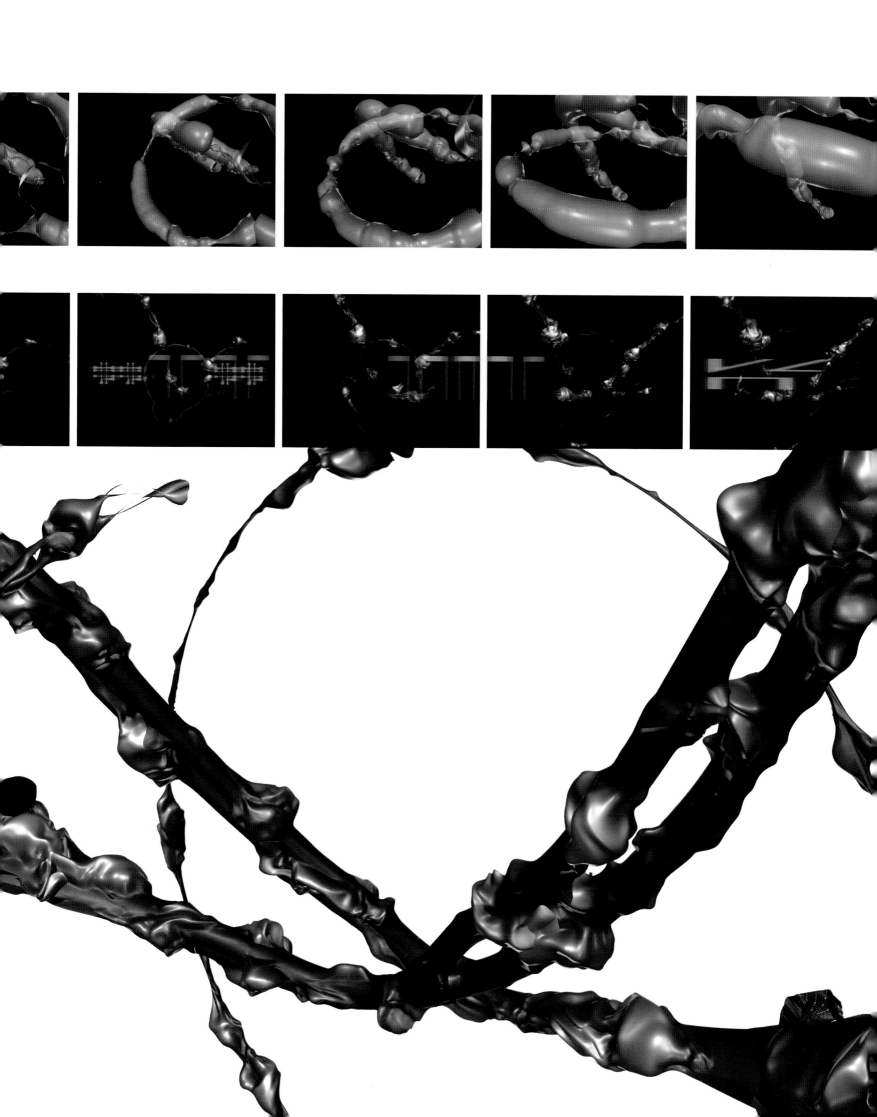

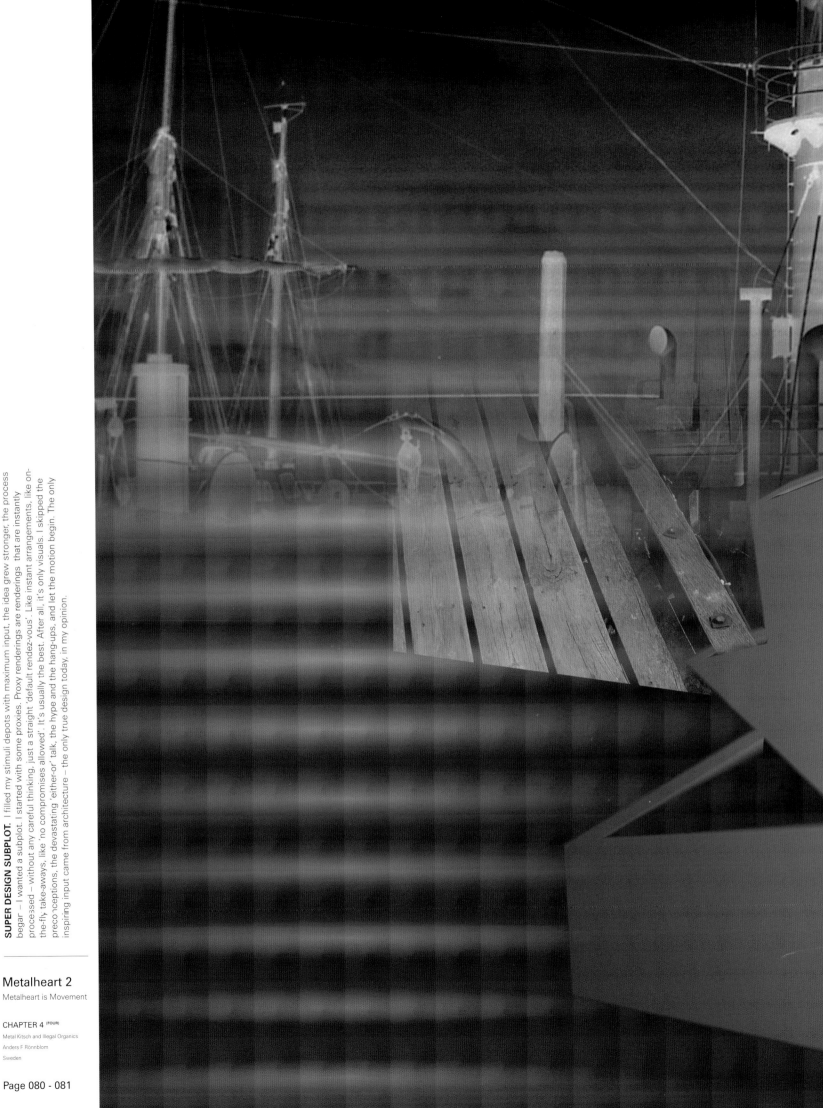

SUPER DESIGN SUBPLOT. I filled my stimuli depots with maximum input, the idea grew stronger, the process began – I wanted a subplot. I started with some proxies. Proxy renderings are renderings that are instantly processed – without any careful thinking, just a straight 'default rendez-vous'. Like instant arrangements, like on-the-fly take-aways, like 'no compromises allowed'. It's usually the best. After all, it's only visuals. I skipped the preco nceptions, the devastating 'either-or' talk, the hype and the hang-ups, and let the motion begin. The only inspiring input came from architecture – the only true design today, in my opinion.

Metalheart 2

Metalheart is Movement

CHAPTER 4 (FOUR)

Metal Kitsch and Illegal Organics
Anders F Rönnblom
Sweden

SUB:TRAC:TION PLOTS

IMATED MBPS AT ... TO SERVE: 56243.89 MODEM GAIN AND CONVERTED: 452.876 AT WBPS 20 ... FUL

ANDERS F RÖNNBLOM: SUPER DESIGN SUBPLOT – the working title for a MetalHeart CD-Rom project, produced by Studio Matchbox for Agosto Inc., Tokyo. The original Super Design Subplot collection incluc

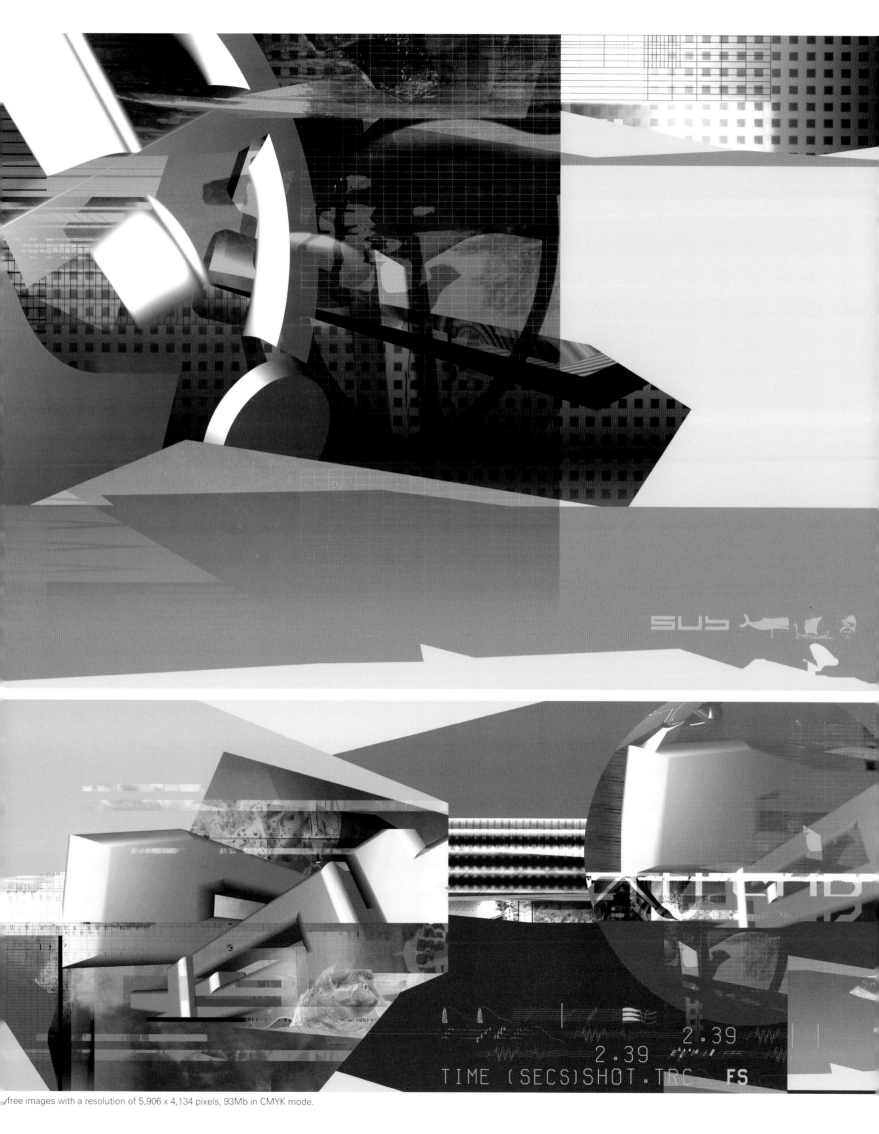

Metalheart 2

Metalheart is Movement

CHAPTER 4 (FOUR)

Metal Kitsch and Illegal Organics

Anders F Rönnblom

Sweden

SUPER DESIGN SUBPLOT FRAMES.

I shot a good hundred digital pictures of streets and statues and merged them with 3D objects of metallic substance. This was my way of saying: "Graphic Design is no more." I wanted to build another world of bodies. I'm still here shooting night scenes for another conspiracy project. I guess it will be 'sub-this' or 'sub that'. I don't want it to be busy and overworked, and I don't want it to be simple and clean. I just want the graphics to be submaximal. Screen dumps from heaven. I could print them out throw them in the air like confetti, shoot some DV footage, take them back to the computer and make the ultimate subplot compositing. That's all.

Metalheart 2
Metalheart is Movement

CHAPTER 5 (FIVE)
Metalheart is a Growing Community
Global Contributions II

Page 086 - 087

METALHEART IS A GROWING COMMUNITY
Global contributions II

Metalheart is growing. We clearly see the
Metalheart concept branching out and includ-
ing a broader spectrum of digital art. Graphic
designers are making stunning 2D animations.
Illustrators are becoming spectacular 3D
animators. Photographers are creating video
art. Art Directors are successful filmmakers.
Commercial or non-commercial. Traditional cuts
or experimental blends.

This chapter includes a mixture of 'Classic
Metalheart' illustrations and a more traditional
style of fine art photography and image manipulations all imbedded in a typical 'Touch of
Metalheart'.

Artists included in the 'Global Contributions II' section:

Lou Zadesky, USA	Ted Kapke, USA
Kalle Everland, Sweden	R.R. Tidd, USA
Per Gustafson, Sweden	André Sanchez, France
Stéphane Faure, France	Christine Plican, Canada
Jens Karlsson , Sweden	Daniel Long, USA
James Widegren, Sweden	Dave Taylor, USA
Hugo O. Delevante, Canada	Filippo Spiezia, Italy
Richard Krall, USA	Michael Knight, Canada
Charlie Owens, USA	Halvor Bodin, Norway
Robert Zohrab, New Zealand	Maja Rapetskaja, USA
Eric Schumacher, USA	Klas Tauberman, Sweden
Sergio Spada, Italy	D-FUSE, England
Hugh Sicotte, USA	Dan Talson, England
Raj Naik, USA	Hector Ramirez, USA
Cameron Redwine, USA	Thomas Sandrock, USA
James Marsden, England	Laura Alexander, USA
Hiroshi Kunoh, Japan	Torgeir Holm, Norway
Viktor Koen, USA	Mattias Lindberg, Sweden
Dessie Alessandro, USA	Klas Jonsson, Sweden
Gülnur Güvenç, Turkey	Alessandro Bavari, Italy
Jim Sincock, USA	Suk & Koch, USA

LOU ZADESKY is a freelance artist who runs his own design studio, Screaming Cactus, in San Francisco, California. He specializes in print and web-related design using a variety of 2D and 3D programs, such as Photoshop, 3D Studio Max and After Effects, and he is currently adding live video footage to his online work. Lou was also represented in the first Metalheart book. **E-mail:** lou@screamingcactus.com **URL:** www.screamingcactus.com

Metalheart 2

Metalheart is Movement

CHAPTER 5 (FIVE)

Global Contributions II

Lou Zadesky

USA

66

Sometimes I feel like shit so don't waste my fuckin time
I don't need no family just a big fat check of royalties

I know what I wanna do but I just don't seem to get it through and I can't do anything

You live like a wanna-be in this sick society and your sitting next to me
can't you fucking see I know how I ended up here

Suck your piece of shit for real and I can't do anything

Design: Lou Zadesky

I gotta go now, and I don't need you. Sometimes it feels like suicide it's on my mind. I ain't got time for a second round.
I gotta go go go 'til I find that piece of mind.

And I hate you and I can break you. Sometimes you have to realize that I ain't nice. I had to break that bitch for a second time.
I gotta go go go 'til I find that piece of mind.

And I ain't takin' more of your good advise. I wanna feel like I'm supernatural one more time. But I dought I'm gonna be old.
You know I had to please my soul. Somehow you feel like me, so why don't we drop it.

-Borg, Dregen, Carlsson

metalheart

metalheart
a brainpasta imbax project

metalheart is love : metalheart is the description of a process, not of a result
passion of digital design is based on the power of the pixel : the power of noise and fractals
the power of layers and channels : the power of using blending calculations : the power of 3D

I don't care what you say cause I'm born to lose and I don't give a damn if I'm a fool for you.
Look out! All messed up this time cause I've been walking 'round with myself. I'm just a deadend creeper.
Didn't mind to wait it now it's happened to me all over again.

Somewhere deep inside there's a neon sign tells me where to ride man when I'm bombed out of my mind.

I was desperate for a place to put out my cigarette. I found love in the nick of time, and that is something that I really
don't have but now I don't care if I live or die man.

You wanna come over with me.
You wanna ride with me.
You wanna blow this town cause I don't got time to show you.

All my secrets are buried down here and I will show them if you want me to,
a white night space racer in sight it's so beautiful with noise and height.

-Iggy Stages, Curtain

METALHEART by LOU ZADESKY – This series of experimental animations are made paying particular attention to the ambient and diffuse properties of reflection, refraction and opacity settings. Please view the movies at www.screamingcactus.com/metal/

KALLE EVERLAND is a new media designer currently residing in Stockholm, Sweden. After working as a graphic designer at Real Life Production, he is now freelancing through the freelance network ReStructure. On his spare time he manages SPLSH.COM which is his creative outlet for onscreen productions. He enjoys working on huge print spreads while listening to Britney Spears and drink way too much coffee. Kalle was also represented in the first Metalheart book. **Xenomorph** – Inspired by the 'Alien' movies, a visualization of the phrase 'organic metal'. **Microprobe** – This piece aims to illustrate nanotechnology, I've always been intrigued by microworlds, worlds that exists inside particles, circuits, etc. **E-mail:** kalle@splsh.com **URL:** www.SPLSH.COM

SPLSH.COM
VISUAL RESEARCH & DEVELOPMENT

DMX.TECHNOLOGY

XENOMORPH

Metalheart 2
Metalheart is Movement

CHAPTER 5 (FIVE)
Global Contributions II
Kalle Everland
Sweden

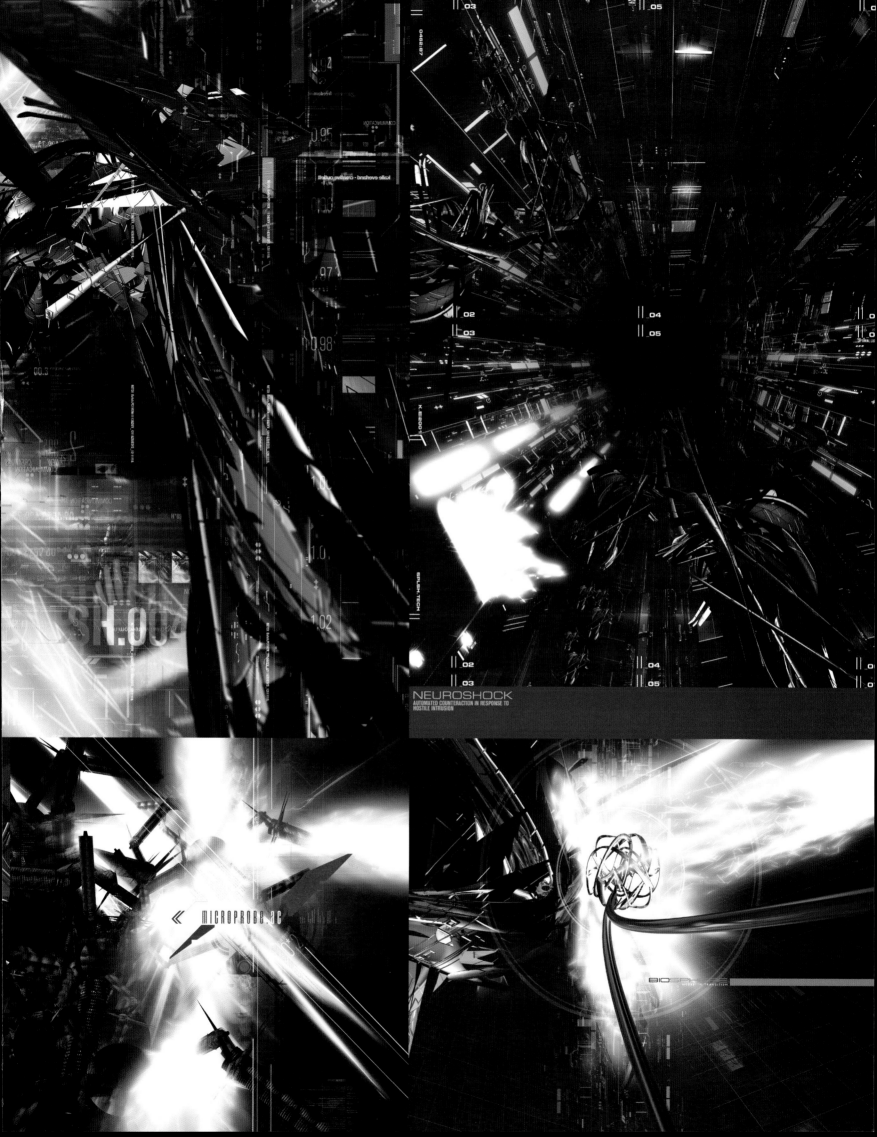

NEUROSHOCK
AUTOMATED COUNTERACTION IN RESPONSE TO
HOSTILE INTRUSION

MICROPROBE.36

BIOSPHERE

MODULAR TECHNOLOGY 357
MODULAR.TECHNOLOGY

KALLE EVERLAND: Modular technology –
Originally created for a book project called
'Real Life Design Report, exploration of light
and asymmetry'.

Metalheart 2
Metalheart is Movement

CHAPTER 5 (FIVE)
Global Contributions II
Kalle Everland
Sweden

METALHEART IS ART... THIS IS ART · · ·   03.8996

PER GUSTAFSON I MODERNSTYLE.NU

ASTROBUGS METALHEART.02

53.796

PER GUSTAFSON is a 22 year old graphic designer from Sweden, who currently works in the Internet-based company 'geidemark gustafson' (geidemarkgustafson.nu), and who is also the founder of the experimental design studio online called MODERNSTYLE.NU. Per was also represented in the first Metalheart book, and Astrobugs' is a 300 dpi image especially engineered for the Metalheart 2 book, created early in 2002.
E-mail: pege_one@yahoo.com **URL:** www.modernstyle.nu

Metalheart 2
Metalheart is Movement

CHAPTER 5 (FIVE)
Global Contributions II
Per Gustafsson
Sweden

Page 096 - 097

STÉPHANE FAURE is a 25 year old digital designer from the city of Le Pless s-Bouchard in France. He is a graphic design student and works on the PC platform with Photoshop, Illustrator, Bryce and Poser, Director and Flash. **Email:** stephane.sf.faure@wanadoo.fr

Metalheart 2

Metalheart is Movement

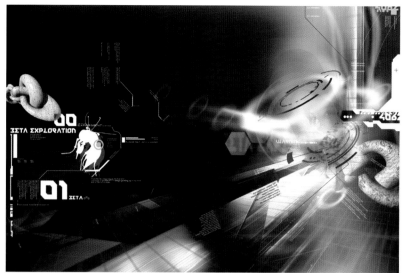
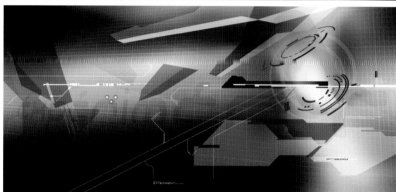

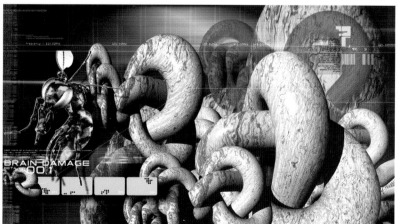

JENS KARLSSON is a Swedish graphic designer, who is actively involved in enriching the online design culture with news, articles, and events, mainly as assistant creative director at www.threeoh.com. Jens was also represented in the first Metalheart book. **E-mail:** jens@Chapter3.net **URL:** www.Chapter3.net

Acclaimed Swedish designer **JAMES WIDEGREN** is the driving force behind the cult design site threeoh.com, a forum for the promotion of well-designed communications media. **URL:** www.threeoh.com   www.idiocase.com

HUGO O. DELEVANTE is running HOD Studio, a Canadian team of graphic artists and animators with the philosophy 'Think Novel'. Mixing 2D and 3D for graphic design and virtual design concepts, Hod Studio is producing corporate design, video clips and interactive web sites. **E-mail:** hodstudio@hodstudio.com **URL:** www.hodstudio.com

Metalheart 2
Metalheart is Movement

CHAPTER 5 (FIVE)

Global Contributions II

Jens Karlsson / James Videgren

Sweden

Hugo O. Delevante, Canada

'Digital Dominion' is a collaboration between **JENS KARLSSON** and **JAMES WIDEGREN**.

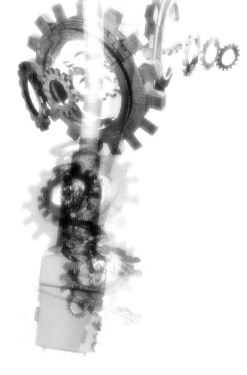

HUGO O. DELEVANTE

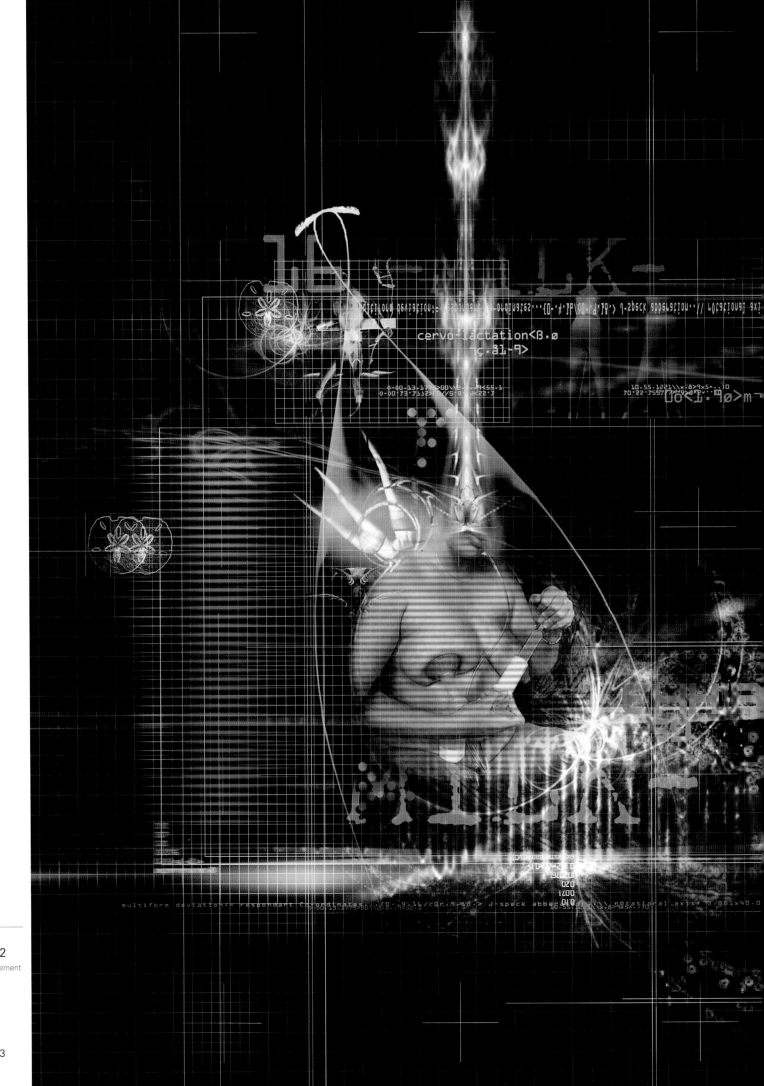

RICHARD KRALL is a graphic designer from New York.
Richard was also represented in the first Metalheart book.
E-mail: dixpix@earthlink.net

Metalheart 2

Metalheart is Movement

CHAPTER 5 (FIVE)

Global Contributions II

Richard Krall

USA

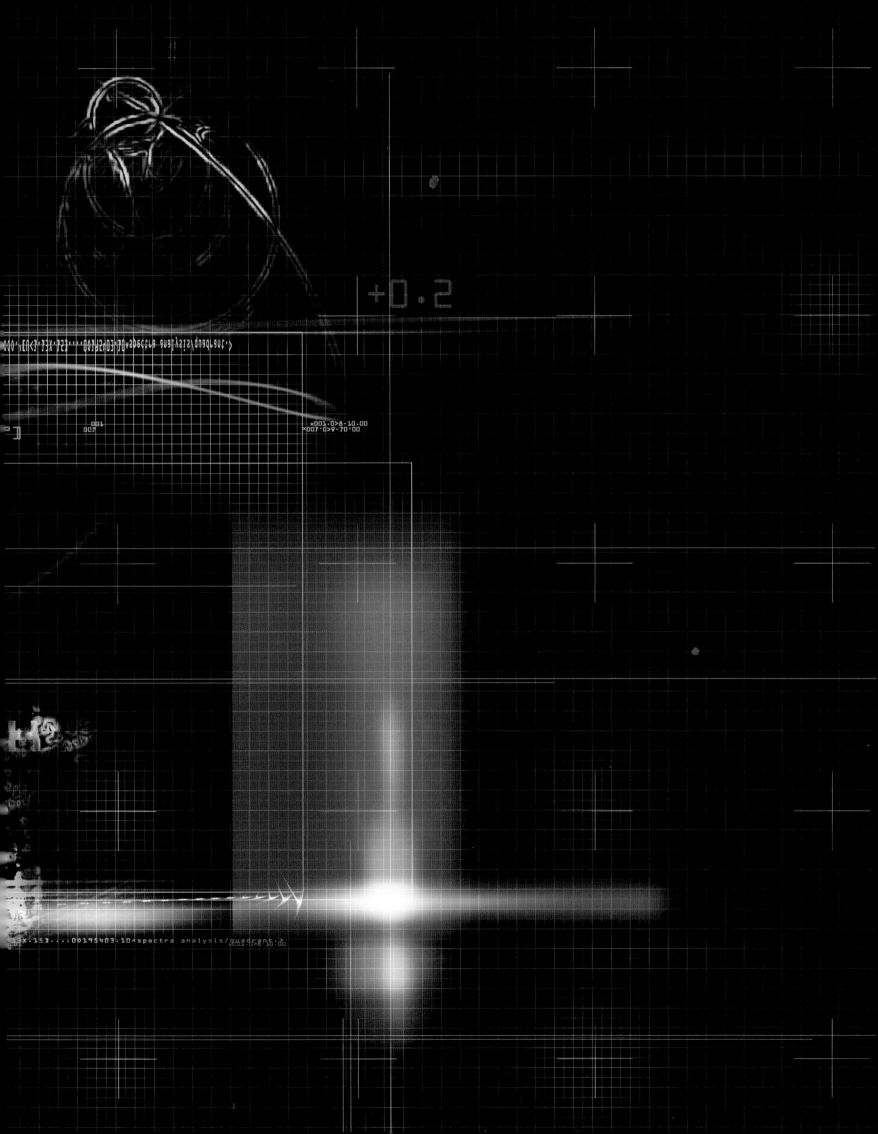

FUNCTIONONE▼

F
1

FAILURE

BLOODSTAINED

SICKBASTARD.ATL.GA.30324.B12.USA.K.TN.5.19.74.27.

CHARLIE OWENS is a digital designer from Atlanta, Georgia.
Titles: 'Function' and 'Bloodstain'. **E-mail:** chuk@twitchco.com

Metalheart 2
Metalheart is Movement

CHAPTER 5 (FIVE)
Global Contributions II
Charlie Owens
USA

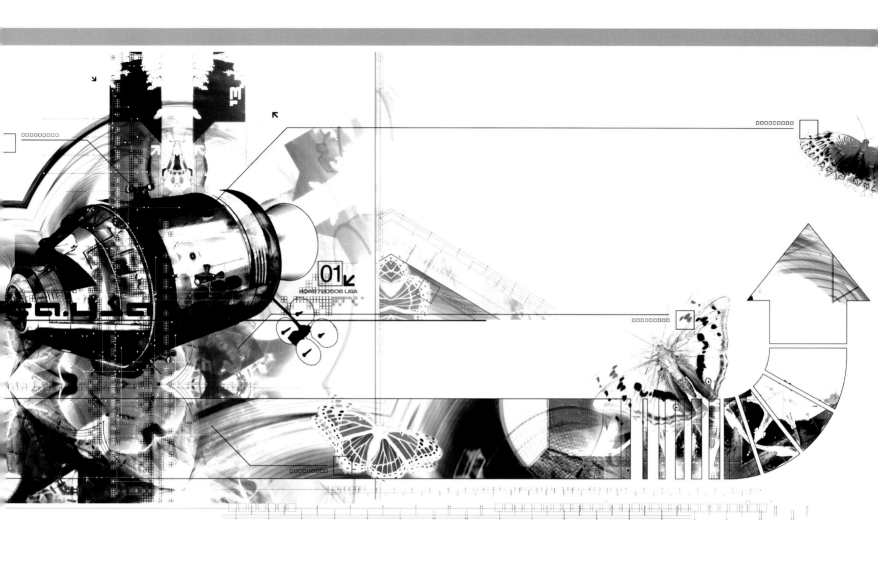

01 ↙
4048720508 USA

SICKBASTARD

02.06.02 VERSION 06.
51974B12ATL

02.06.02 VERSION 06

BLOODSTAINED
SHE WILL NOT BE SO LUCKY
HAVE MY SHOES ONCE AGAIN

TO BE 02 ↙

SICKBASTARD
travis 51974b12.ca

SHE BEAT ME WITH MY OWN SHOES
THE STORY OF FREDDY THE FISH

ONCE WHEN I WAS A POOR JEWISH BOY
LIVING IN THE DARK COLD MOUNTAINS OF
ALASKA I HAD A PET FISH THAT I FEED IN
MY HOUSE EVERYDAY I WOULD FEED HIM
FOOD FROM MY MOTHERS TABLE
WHEN SHE FOUND THIS OUT SHE TOOK
MY SHOES AWAY SO I COULD NOT WALK
THROUGH THE SNOW TO GET MY PET
FISH BUT I WOULD STILL GO EVERYDAY
AND I FEED MY FISH WOULD BE WAITING
ON THE ONE DAY I WENT TO THE RIVER TO
FEED MY FISH AND HE WAS NOT THERE I
WAITED UNTIL MY FEET COULD NOT
TAKE IT ANYMORE

WHEN I RETURNED TO MY HOUSE
MY MOTHER WAS LAUGHING AND LOOKING
AT HER FINGERS FROM THE LEFT OVERS
OF THE MEAL WE HAD EATEN BEFORE I WENT
TO THE RIVER MY FISH WAS DEAD SHE STARTED
ME THAT WEEK AND EATEN HIM FOR LUNCH THEN
ME THAT WEEK AND THE REMAINS OF MY LUNCH IN
MY POCKET FOR MY FRIEND

02.
SHE WILL NOT BE SO LUCKY AND I WILL
HAVE MY SHOES ONCE AGAIN
BLOODSTAINED
AND I FINISHED MY LUNCH

twitch.51974.B12.30324atlgausa

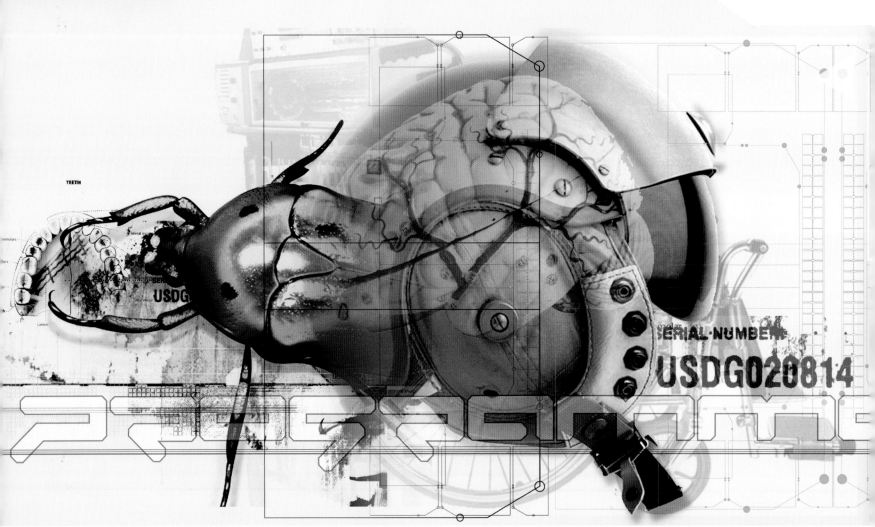

Metalheart 2
Metalheart is Movement

'A BUG'S LIFE' and 'PROGRAMMED' by **CHARLIE OWENS**

CHAPTER 5 (FIVE)
Global Contributions II
Charlie Owens
USA

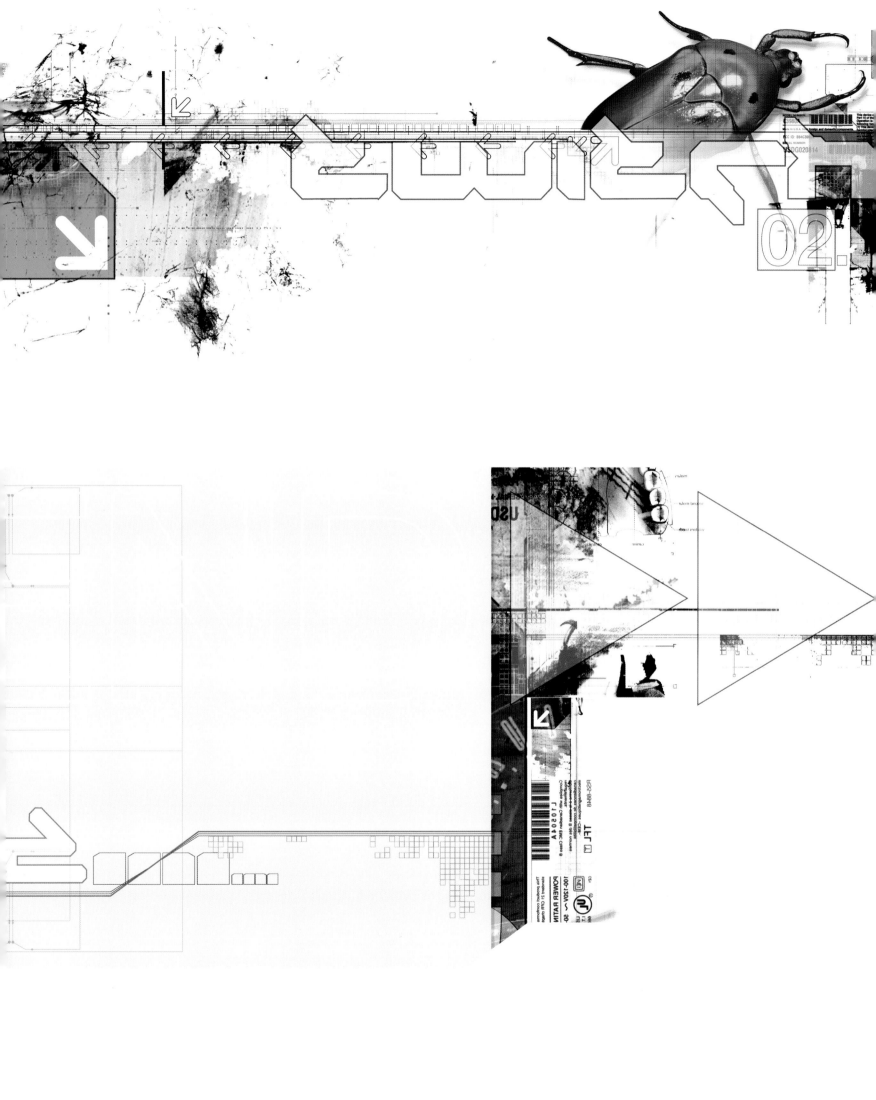

HYbBRRIiD

20TH:OCTOBER
GALATOS

ROBERT ZOHRAB is a graphic designer from Auckland, New Zealand. working with flyers and record covers and video live art performances. Robert was also represented in the first Metalheart book.
E-mail: cybcult@ihug.co.nz URL: www.cyberculture.co.nz

Metalheart 2
Metalheart is Movement

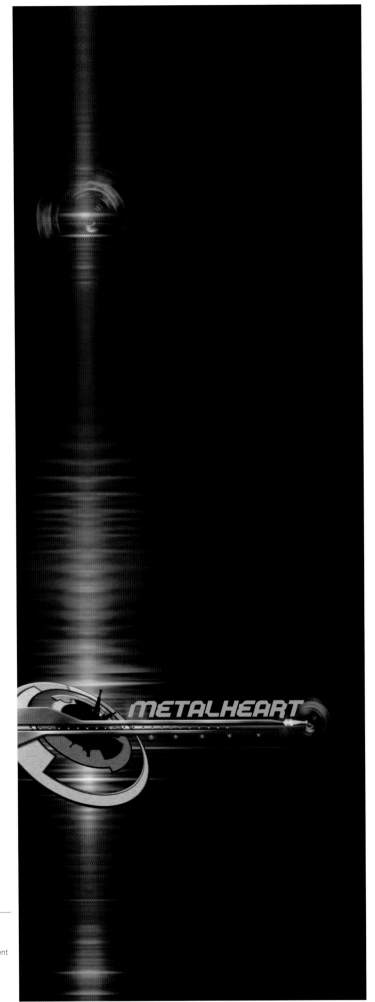

ERIC SCHUMACHER

SERGIO SPADA

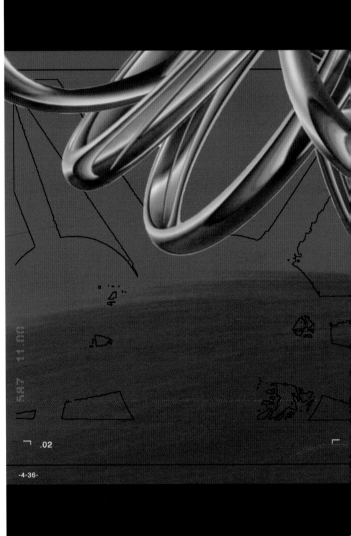

HUGH SICOTTE

ERIC SCHUMACHER is a digital artist from San Francisco, USA. **Email:** schuuu@eartlink.net
SERGIO SPADA is a digital artist from Udine in Italy, specializing in enhanced imaging, illustration and art. **Email:** spadacom@spa-da.com
HUGH SICOTTE is a digital artist from Brooklyn, New York, focusing on dynamic web design.
E-mail : hugh@upstarsrecords.com

Metalheart 2
Metalheart is Movement

CHAPTER 5 (FIVE)

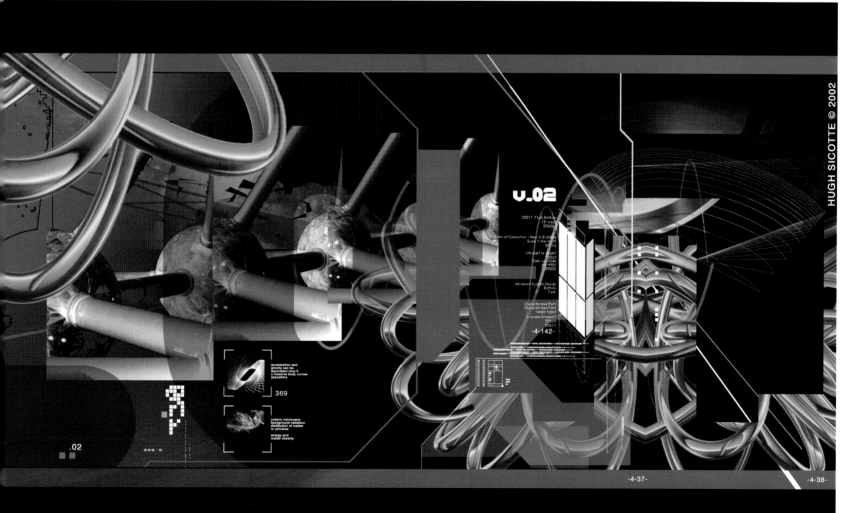

v.02

acceleration and
gravity can be
equivalent only if
a massive body curves
spacetime

369

cosmic microwave
background radiation
distribution of matter
in universe

energy and
matter density

.02

www.rajnaik.com

graphic design
photography
advertising

DIGITAL ART & DESIGN
raj.n

2002: metalheart in motion

the power of the pixel, the power of noise & fractals

METALHEART
2002: METALHEART IN MOTION

RAJ NAIK is based in Los Angeles, California, and his clients include many record companies. He works with a variety of software programs, such as Photoshop, Illustrator, Bryce, After Effects, Flash, Dreamweaver, and ProTools for multimedia/audio.
E-mail: raj@netwood.net   URL: www.rajnaik.com

Metalheart 2
Metalheart is Movement

CHAPTER 5 (FIVE)
Global Contributions II
Raj Naik
USA

METALHEART 2

2002 METALHEART IN MOTION

RAJ.NAIK

WWW.RAJNAIK.COM

graphic design
advertising
photography

CAMERON REDWINE, based in Atlanta, Georgia, is working with promotion-related graphics for raves, clubs, pubs and bars – basically music and night life. Software used: Photoshop, Illustrator, and Bryce. Robert was also represented in the first Metalheart book.
E-mail: cameron@one3.com

Metalheart 2
Metalheart is Movement

CHAPTER 5 (FIVE)
Global Contributions II
Cameron Redwine
USA

J.P.M. 2001.

Metalheart 2
Metalheart is Movement

JAMES MARSDEN is a British digital artist. Titles: 'GRAFIK FIRECRACKERS', 'HERB', 'PURPLE EYES' and 'THE SOUL PT.2'.
E-mail: jamars@madfish.com **URL:** www.jpm-grafik.co.uk

CHAPTER 5 (FIVE)
Global Contributions II
James Marsden
England

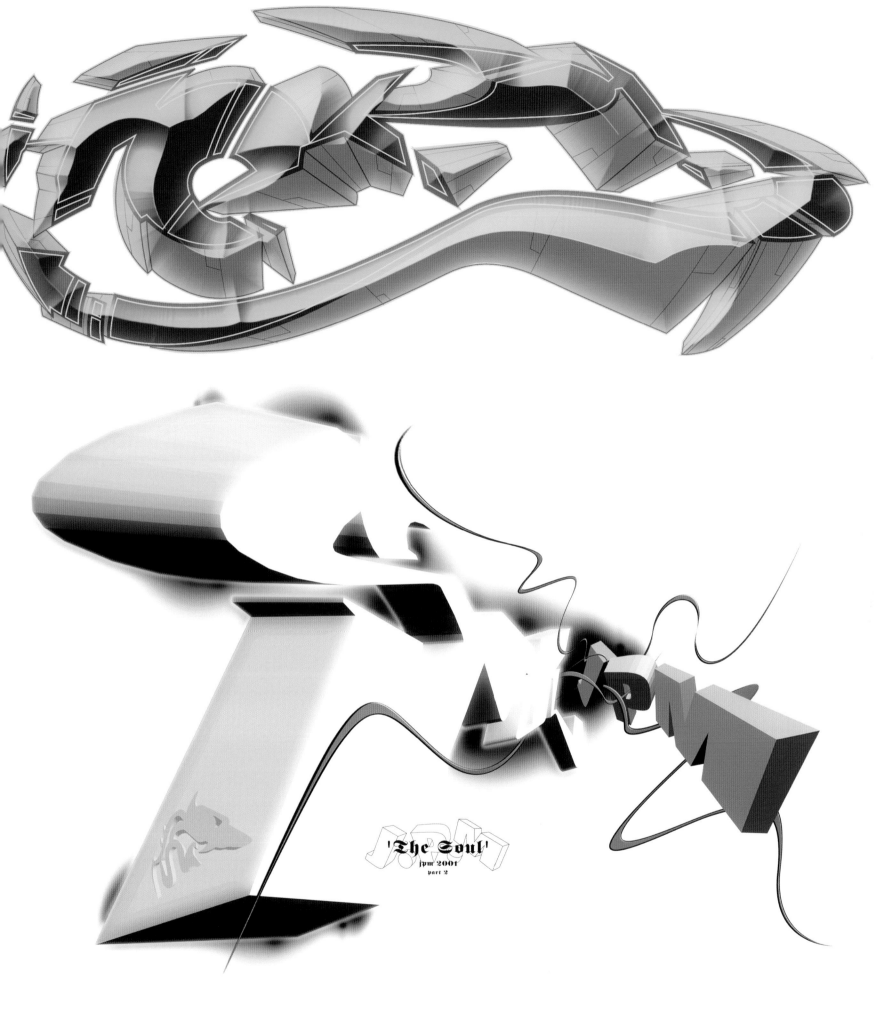

'The Soul'
jrm 2001
part 2

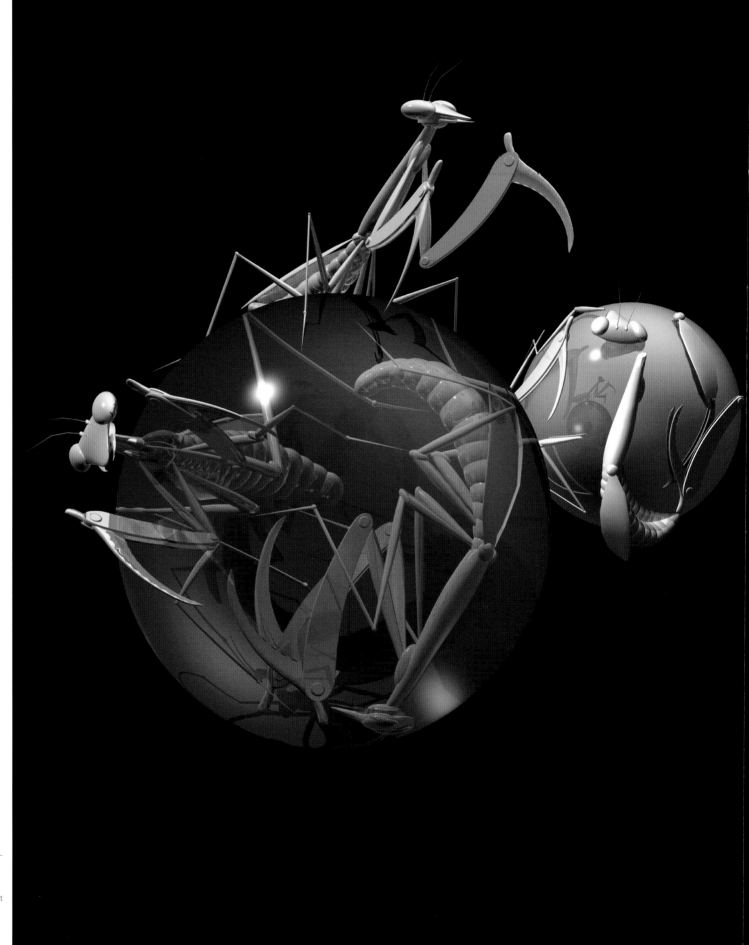

HIROSHI KUNOH is a Japanese digital artist who is using Strata Studio Pro to create exciting 3D illustrations of animals and plants.
E-mail: kunoh@silver.ocn.ne.jp

Metalheart 2

Metalheart is Movement

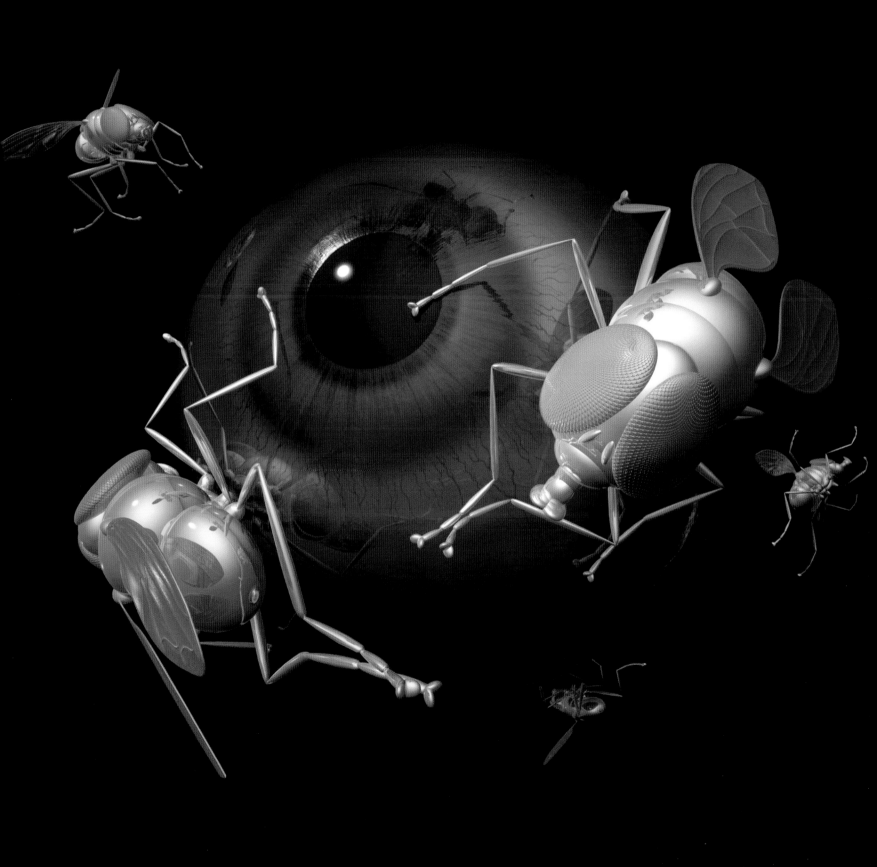

VIKTOR KOEN is a renowned and awarded digital artist from New York City, who is specializing in image montages. Viktor was one of the nominees to the Digital Hall of Fame Award 2001. E-mail: viktor@viktorkoen.com URL: www.viktorkoen.com
DESSIE ALESSANDRO runs the Chicago-based multimedia design studio Eminus3, together with Mehvash Farrukh. Dessie is currently working with photographer Jason Imber on a show titled 'Femalemonsters'.
E-mail: eminus3designlab@mindspring.com URL: www.eminus3.com

Metalheart 2
Metalheart is Movement

CHAPTER 5 (FIVE)
Global Contributions II
Viktor Koen, USA
Dessie Alessandro, USA

Page 120 - 121

VIKTOR KOEN

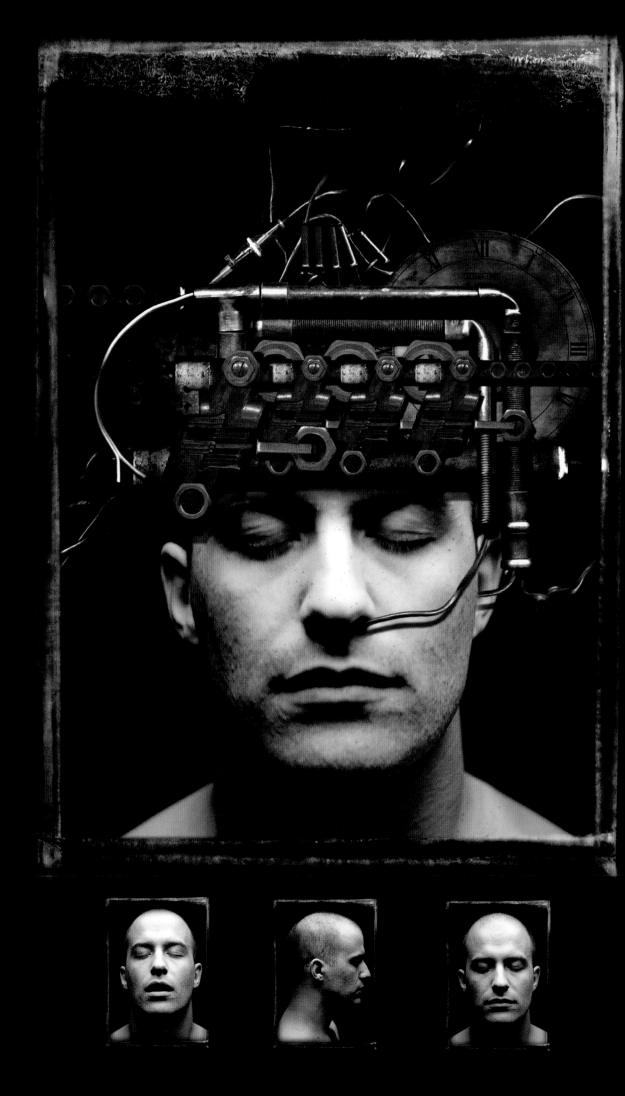

GÜLNUR GÜVENÇ is a freelance artist from Ankara, Turkey, who has worked as an architect for more than ten years. In her photographic manipulations she chooses to make minor touches among numerous possibilities offered by the software, as she prefers to develop a personal style based on her interests and sensibilities, rather than a visual style based on the possibilities offered by filters and plugins.
E-mail: gulguvenc@ttnet.net.tr **URL:** www.gulguvenc.com

Metalheart 2
Metalheart is Movement

CHAPTER 5 (FIVE)
Global Contributions II
Gulner Güvenç
Turkey

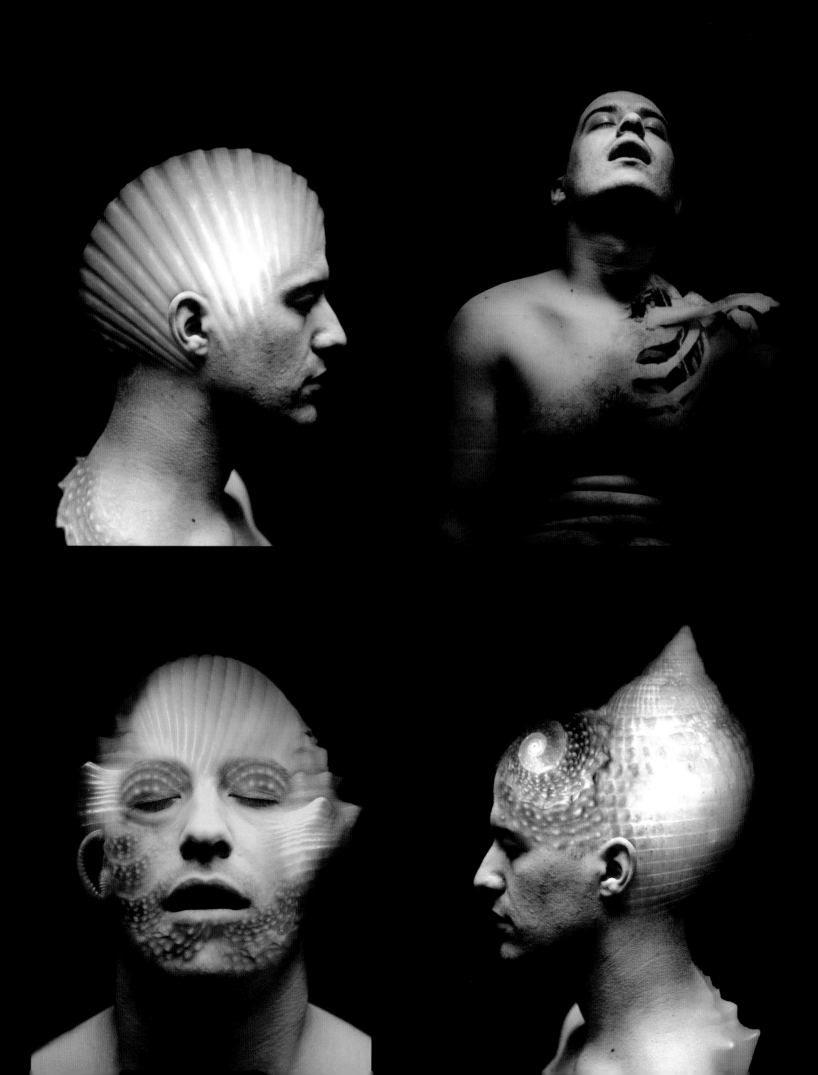

JIM SINCOCK, located in Boulder, Colorado, is a commercial photographer who has been brought back to his fine art background. The discovery of the program Live Picture many years ago helped him to change the way he creates his images. Starting with traditional photography, images are scanned and tweaked in Photoshop and then composed in Live Picture on his Mac G3. Jim created the 'Interrobang' site in 1998 as an outlet for his artier and less commercial works. Since then he has added like-minded artists R.R. Tidd and Tod Kapke (see page 126-129). While they each run their own photography businesses, they work together under the Interrobang name to help promote each other's art.
E-mail: jim@interrobang.org **URL:** www.interrobang.org

Metalheart 2

Metalheart is Movement

CHAPTER 5 (FIVE)

Global Contributions II

Jim Sincock

USA

TED KAPKE, located in Boulder, Colorado, is a digital artist and photographer, and a member of the 'Interrobang' design group together with Jim Sincock and R.R. Tidd.
E-mail: ted@interrobang.org **URL:** www.interrobang.org

Metalheart 2
Metalheart is Movement

CHAPTER 5 (FIVE)

Global Contributions II

Ted Kapke

USA

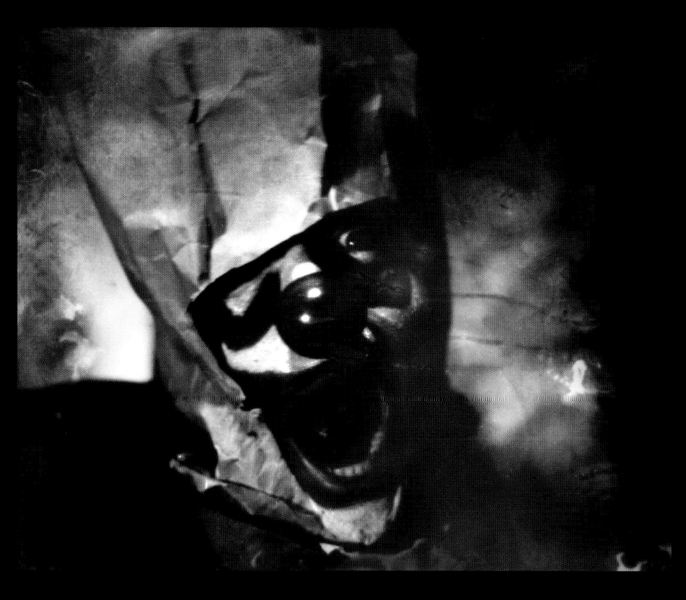

R.R.TIDD. After working for a number of years in the audio-visual and commercial photography industries, honing his skills, R.R.Tidd, from Denver, Colorado, now devotes full attention to fine art – where a mixed media approach, brings more depth to his final images. Working on a Mac G4 with Photoshop and Painter as well as traditional art mediums, gives him the freedom to adlib the images, their themes being created in process.
E-mail: rocky@interrobang.org   **URL:** www.interrobang.org

Metalheart 2

Metalheart is Movement

CHAPTER 5 (FIVE)

Global Contributions II

R. R. Tidd

USA

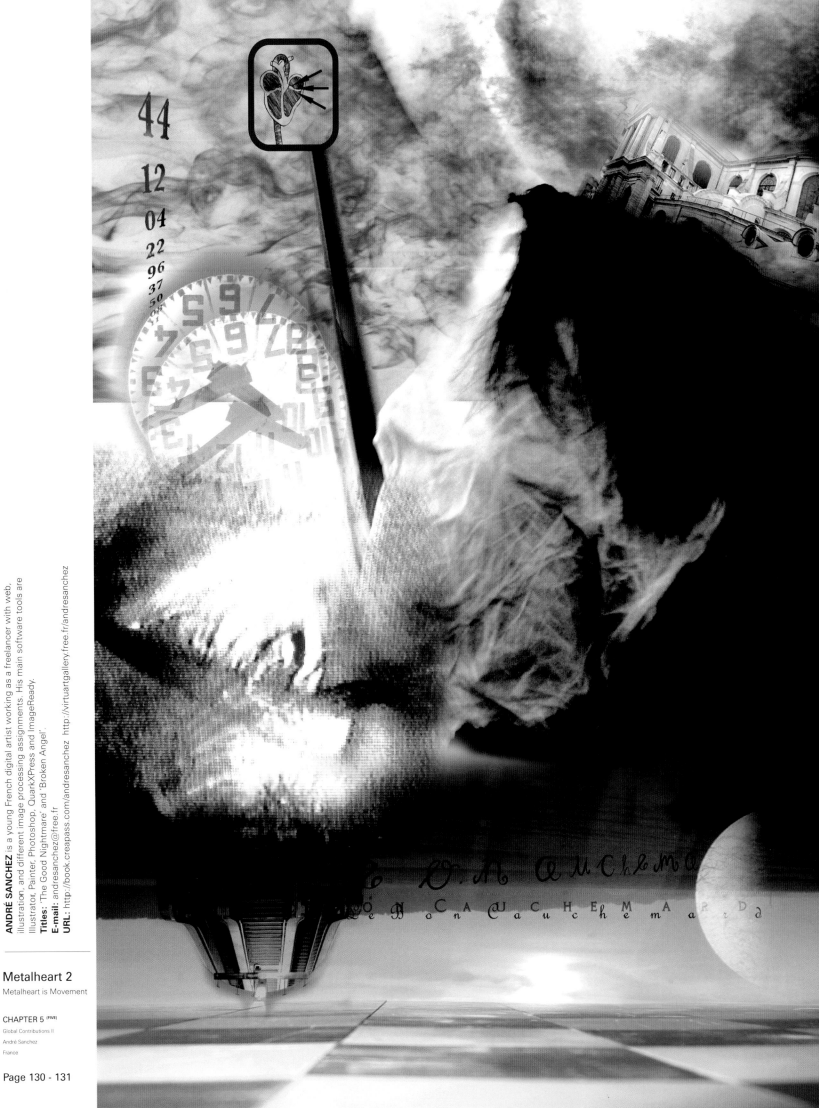

ANDRÉ SANCHEZ is a young French digital artist working as a freelancer with web, illustration, and different image processing assignments. His main software tools are Illustrator, Painter, Photoshop, QuarkXPress and ImageReady.

Titles: 'The Good Nightmare' and 'Broken Angel'.

E-mail: andresanchez@free.fr

URL: http://book.creapass.com/andresanchez http://virtuartgallery.free.fr/andresanchez

Metalheart 2

Metalheart is Movement

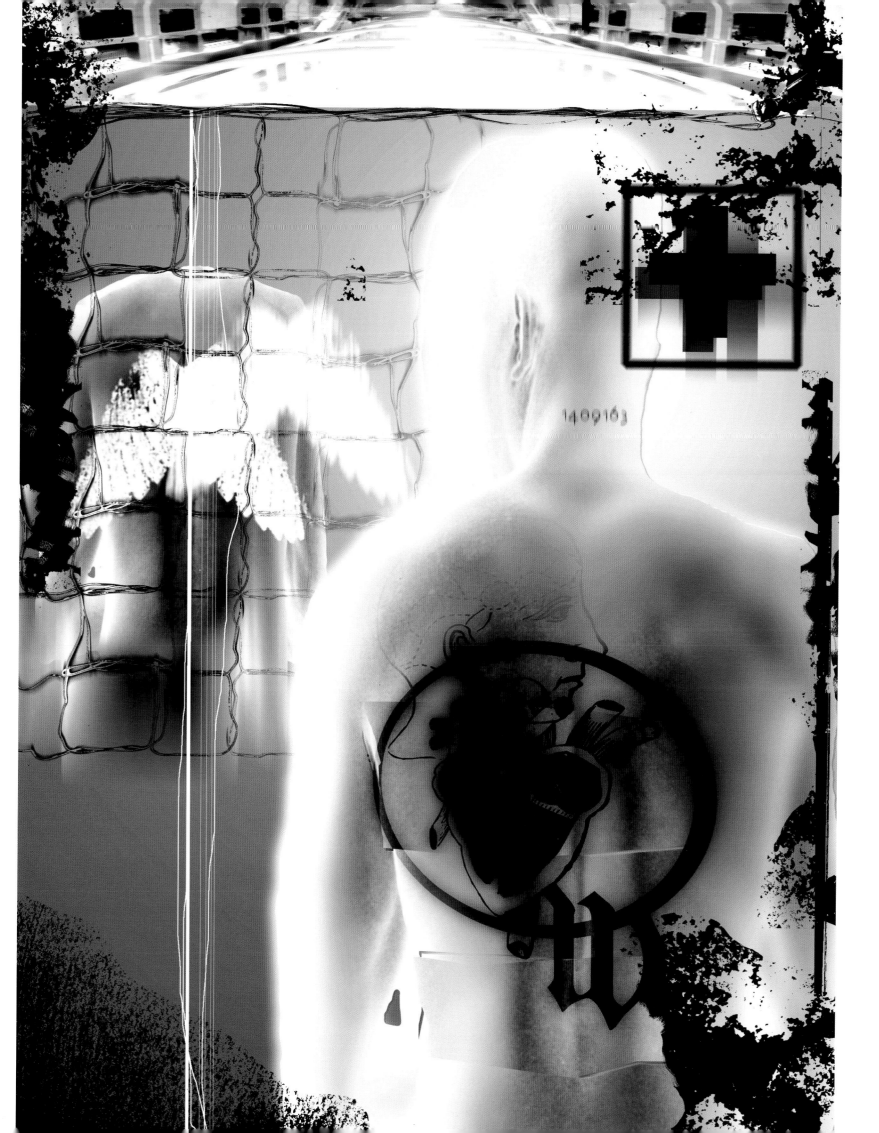

ANDRÉ SANCHEZ, France.
Titles: 'Fair Sex' and 'Black Mask'.

Metalheart 2
Metalheart is Movement

CHAPTER 5 (FIVE)
Global Contributions II
André Sanchez
France

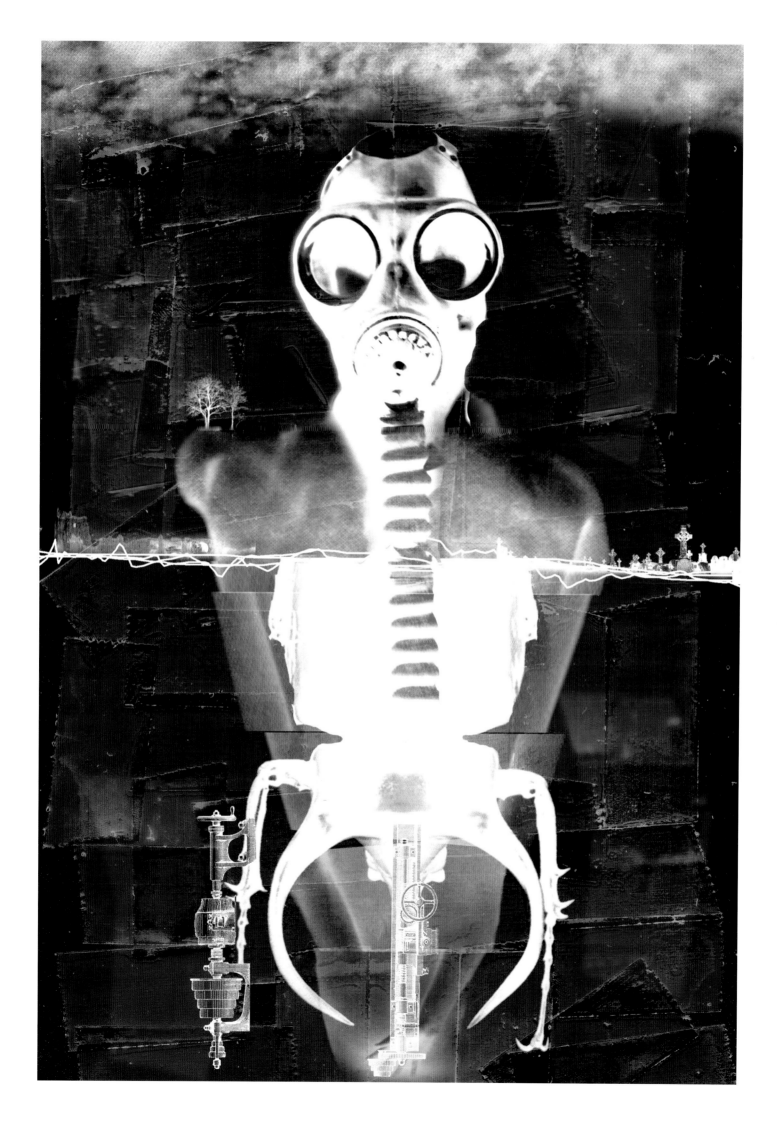

CHRISTINE PLICAN

CHRISTINE PLICAN, digital artist from Edmonton, Canada. **E-mail:** cplican@shaw.ca
DANIEL LONG, digital designer from Washington DC. **E-mail:** daniel@novembre.ws
DAVE TAYLOR, digital artist from Canada. **E-mail:** dave@taylorimaging.com **URL:** www.taylorimaging.com
FILIPPO SPIEZIA, digital designer from Pescara, Italy. **E-mail:** joinfilippo@yahoo.com **URL:** www.filippospiezia.com
MICHAEL D. KNIGHT, digital designer from Winnepeg, Canada. **E-mail:** visual_redemption@yahoo.ca **URL:** visual-redemption.com

Metalheart 2
Metalheart is Movement

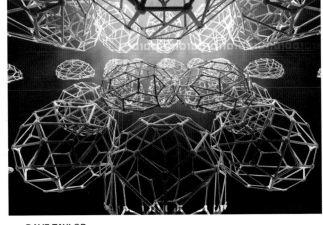

DAVE TAYLOR

FILIPPO SPIEZIA

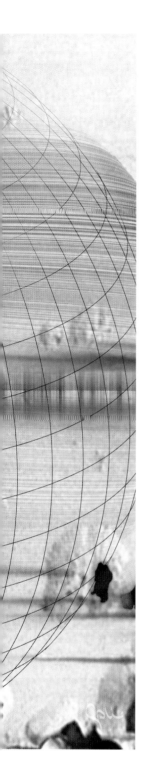

DANIEL LONG

MICHAEL D. KNIGHT

HALVOR BODIN is a graphic designer from Oslo, Norway, who has produced Titles for the feature film PROZAC NATION (I Hate Myself And I Want To Die), released May 2002. Production: Millennium Films. Distribution: Miramax. Directed by: Erik Skjoldbjærg. Cast: Christina Ricci, Jason Biggs, Anne Heche, Michelle Williams, Jonathan Rhys Meyers, Jessica Lange, Nicholas Campbell, Lou Reed. Font: Infinity by Chester & Rick at Thirstype. Photography: Erling Thurmann Andersen.

Title sequence: Animation and design by Halvor Bodin (Virtual Garden, Oslo)

E-Mail: hal@superlow.com **URL:** www.superlow.com   www.virtualgarden.no

Metalheart 2

Metalheart is Movement

CHAPTER 5 (FIVE)

Global Contributions II

Halvor Bodin

Norway

A FILM BY ERIK SKJOLDBJÆRG

ANNE HECHE

MICHELLE WILLIAMS

CASTING BY MARY VERNIEU C.S.A.
ANNE McCARTHY
FELICIA FASANO

CO-PRODUCERS ANDREA SPERLING
CHRISTINA RICCI

CO-PRODUCERS ANDREA SPERLING
CHRISTINA RICCI

EXECUTIVE PRODUCERS WILLI BAER
AVI LERNER
DANNY DIMBORT
TREVOR SHORT
JOHN THOMPSON

SCREENPLAY BY FRANK DEASY
AND LARRY GROSS

DIRECTED BY ERIK SKJOLDBJÆRG

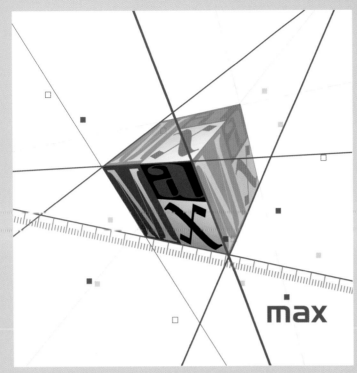

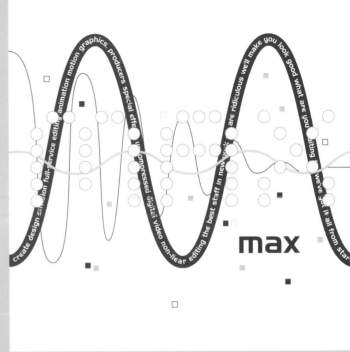

MARIA RAPETSKAJA, Art Director at Maximum Media Productions, a full service broadcast media firm in New Jersey, USA, offering film and video production, animation and graphics. **E-mail:** maria@maximummedia.tv **URL:** www.maximummedia.tv
KLAS TAUBERMAN, digital artist from Stockholm, Sweden. Member of International Style design bureau, focusing on graphic design and 3D for print and web. **E-mail:** klas@thisisis.com **URL:** www.firmadefault.com

Metalheart 2
Metalheart is Movement

CHAPTER 5 (FIVE)
Global Contributions II
Maria Rapetskaja, USA
Klas Tauberman, Sweden

MARIA RAPETSKAJA

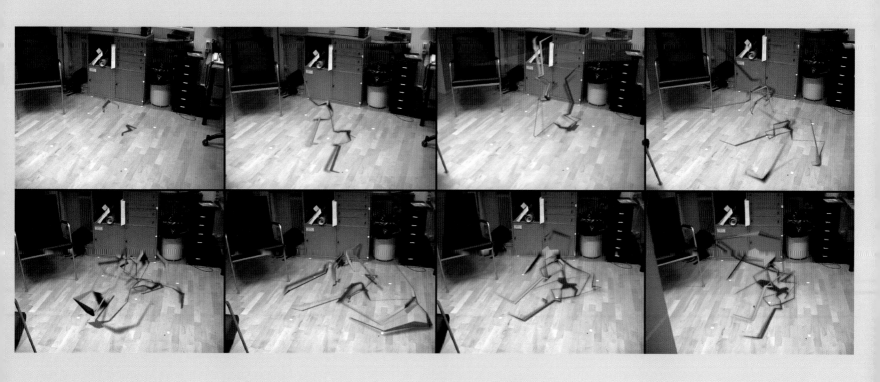

KLAS TAUBERMAN

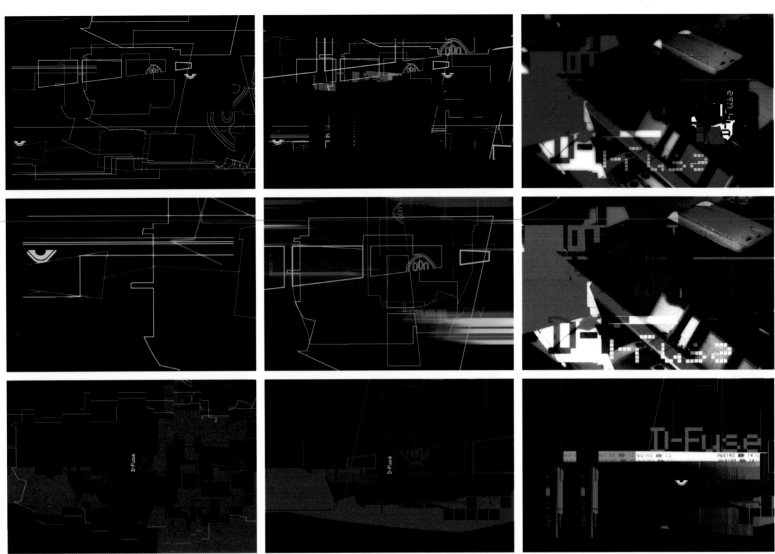

D-FUSE / RAWPAW

DAN TALSON

![Metalheart 2 logo]

Metalheart 2
Metalheart is Movement

CHAPTER 5 (FIVE)

Global Contributions II
D-FUSE / RawPaw, England
Dan Talson, England
Hector Ramirez, USA
Thomas Sandrock, USA
Laura Alexander, USA

D-FUSE / RAWPAW is a design bureau in London, UK, focusing on audiovisual installations and digital filmmaking. **E-mail:** mike@dfuse.com **URL:** www.dfuse.com
DAN TALSON is a digital designer and animator from Herts in England. **E-mail:** dubassy@hotmail.com
LAURA ALEXANDER, from Hoboken, New Jersey, USA, is creating small animations with analogue methods. **E-mail:** laurajoalexander@aol.com
THOMAS SANDROCK is a digital artist from Boulder, Colorado, USA. **E-mail:** tomcat003@angelfire.com **URL:** www.formlesscreative.com
HECTOR RAMIREZ is a digital artist from Chicago, USA. **E-mail:** hekodzine@earthlink.net

 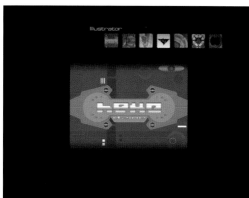 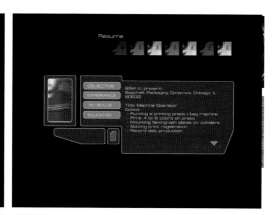

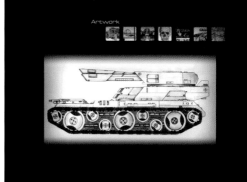 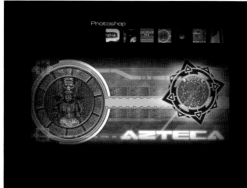 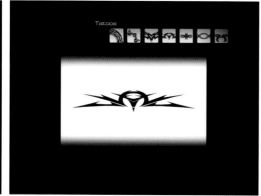

HECTOR RAMIREZ

THOMAS SANDROCK

LAURA ALEXANDER

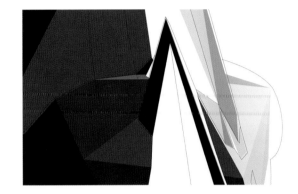

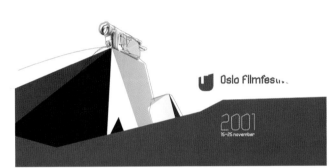

TORGEIR HOLM is a Graphic Designer/Animator and programmer, living and working in Oslo, Norway. Torgeir also made early contributions to the first Metalheart book, and this time his strictly personal style moves dynamically in all directions. **E-Mail:** torgeir@kjeks.nu **URL:** www.kjeks.nu www.egz.com
MATTIAS LINDBERG is a Graphic Designer/Animator from Stockholm, Sweden. His personal digital playground, The SpyBar (www.thespybar.com) and Fakepilot (www.fakepilot.com), are some examples of work he has produced for online purposes. **E-Mail:** mattias@fakepilot.com **URL:** www.fakepilot.com

Metalheart 2
Metalheart is Movement

CHAPTER 5 (FIVE)

Global Contributions II
Torgeir Holm, Norway
Mattias Lindberg, Sweden

Page 142 - 143

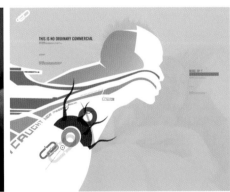

F Oslo Filmfestival

2001
15–25 november

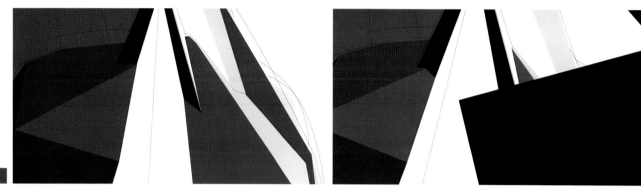

TORGEIR HOLM. The ident for the Oslo Film Festival was created in the following software: 3D Studio Max 4, Illustrator 9, and After Effects 5. The original medium was 35mm film, 2k frames (1.85:1 aspect), 24 fps. The ident was shown directly before all screenings in the festival. Sound: Belplasca prod. Oslo Film Festival profile: Sigurd Kristiansen

MATTIAS LINDBERG. The 44-second Dux commercial was shot with 35mm and a slow-motion camera. The footage was digitized, edited and animated on a PC, using After Effects, Premiere and Photoshop. Flash was used for some of the animations. The shooting session took 2 days, and the editing and animation work was completed in approximately a month.

KLAS JONSSON is a freelance director and designer from Stockholm, Sweden, directing music videos, commercials, and designing main title sequences and animations. He relies heavily on designing advanced sketches in Photoshop, making test renderings in Maya, and delivering very complete and detailed storyboards, before starting to shoot film. Klas works with both DV and 35mm film and is using Final Cut Pro and Adobe After Effects for editing and compositing work. Klas was also represented in the first Metalheart book. **E-mail:** klas.jonsson@swipnet.se **Dream** (title sequence). Client: Finalcut Entertainment. Director/Designer: Klas Jonsson/Strobe. 3D Animator: Robert Karlsson. Producer: Josh Thorne. Post production: The Chimney Pot, Stockholm. Software used: Photoshop, Maya, After Effects. **Triggerhappy:** Writer/Director/Producer/Editor: Klas Jonsson. Director of Photography: Peter Kruse. Visual Effects Supervisor: Robert Karlsson. Visual Effects Animators: Robert Karlsson, Klas Jonsson. Music: Twizt®. Post production: Mancer Post Production. Software used: Photoshop, Illustrator, Maya, After Effects, Final Cut Pro.

Metalheart 2

Metalheart is Movement

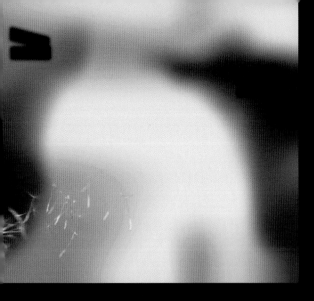

ment

production

edited by

neil farrell

dan farrell

composer and music supervisor

tot taylor

![Metalheart icon] **Metalheart 2**
Metalheart is Movement

ROBERT ZOHRAB is a digital artist from Auckland, New Zealand, running his own studio Hinge Design and specializing in graphic design, web design and CD-Rom production. His most recent projects include DV multimedia projections for outdoor and indoor tech trance festivals, CD/LP cover design, flyer design, logos and motion design for TV. His favorite software programs are: Photoshop, After Effects, and Strata StudioPro. **E-mail:** cybcult@ihug.co.nz **URL:** www.cyberculture.co.nz

CHAPTER 5 (FIVE)

Global Contributions II

Robert Zohrab

New Zealand

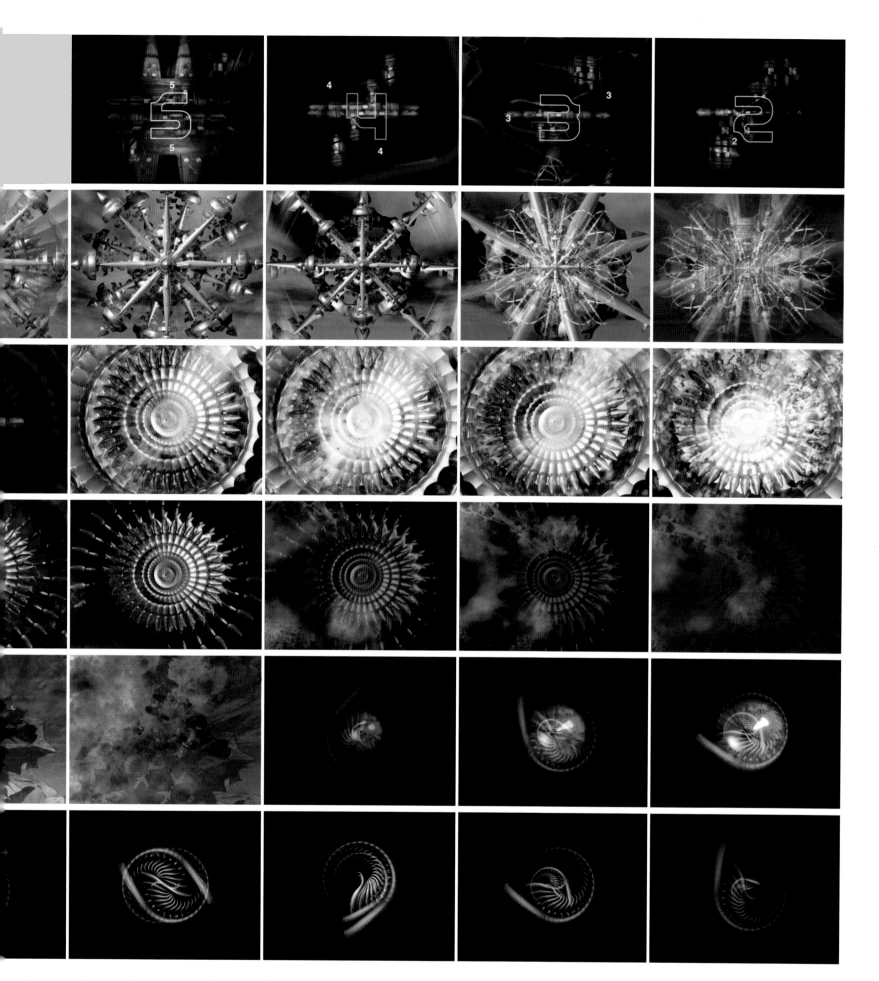

A one minute VJ movie with sound by Artist / Antix : track / Alma

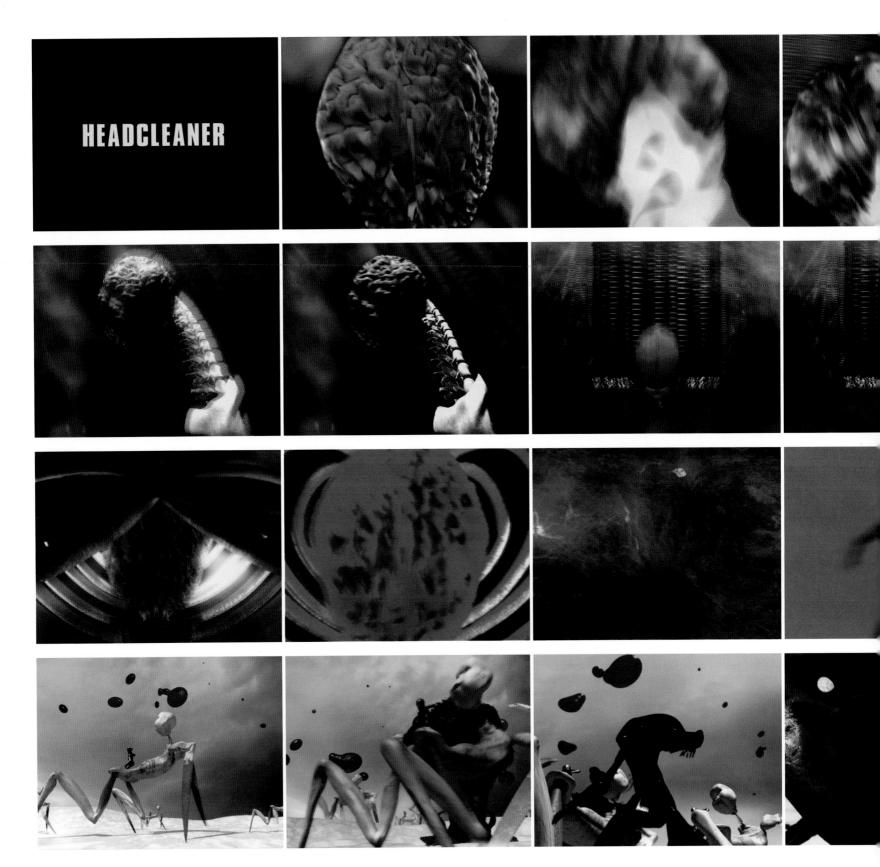

HEADCLEANER

Metalheart 2
Metalheart is Movement

CHAPTER 5 (FIVE)

Global Contributions II

Alessandro Bavari

Italy

Page 148 - 149

ALESSANDRO BAVARI is a renowned graphic designer and animator from Latina, Italy, working with 3D Sudio Max, Photoshop, After Effects and Final Cut Pro. Alessandro has been featured in several international books and magazines and he was honored the Digital Hall of Fame Award 2000 at the 3D Festival in Copenhagen. In 2001 he was nominated with 'Headcleaner' in the 3D Animated Short category, at the 3D Festival Award. **E-mail:** info@alessandrobavari.com **URL:** www.alessandrobavari.com

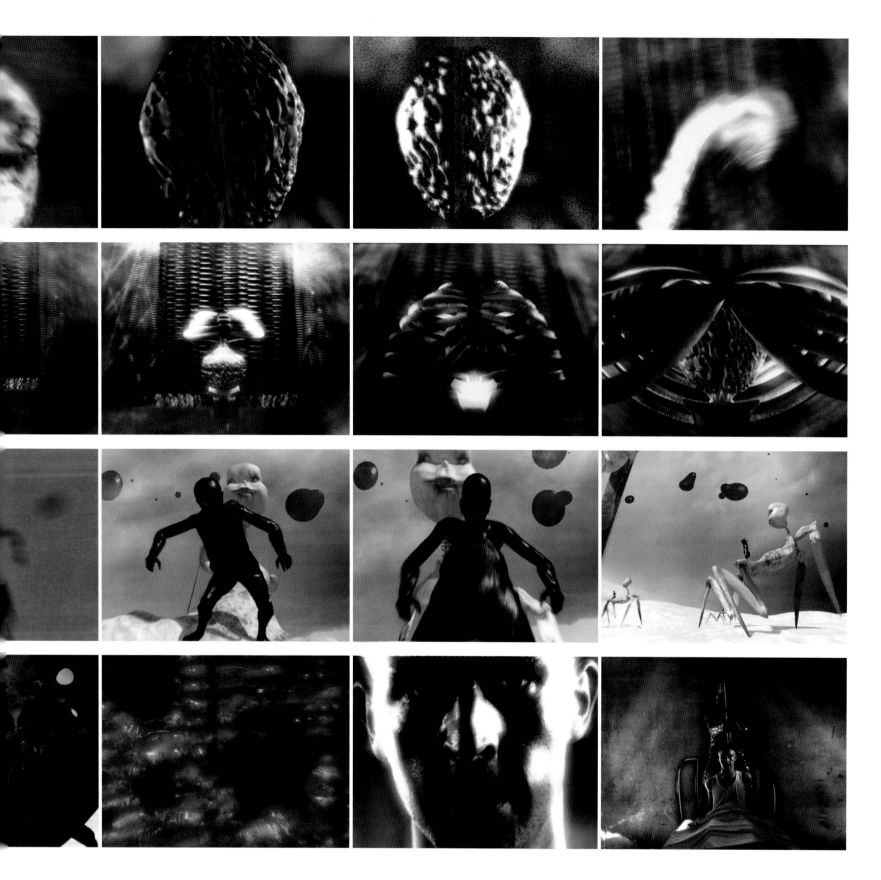

SUK & KOCH Media Inc. is a New York-based motion graphics studio working with experimental art and music videos. **Title:** 'M1NDR3F1LL'.
Year: 2002. Director/Producer/Design/Sound/Music: Suk&Koch. Talent: Kim Min. Production Company: Suk&Koch Media Inc. **Title:** 'IGNORANT'.
Artist: Fuckhead. Director/Producer/Design: Suk&Koch. Type design: Alex Wiederin. Label: Gash Rec. **Title:** 'REPLICA'. Director/Producer/Design/:
Suk&Koch. Art Director: Guenter Eder. Actor: Miye Lee, Uwe Schuster, Phillipe Bastard. Production Company: Suk&Koch Media Inc.
E-mail: sk@sukkoch.com **URL:** www.sukkoch.com

Metalheart 2
Metalheart is Movement

CHAPTER 5 (FIVE)

Global Contributions II
Suk & Koch
USA

MH2

Metalheart 2
Metalheart is Movement

CHAPTER 6 (SIX)
Metalheart is More
The DVD-Rom

Page 152 - 153

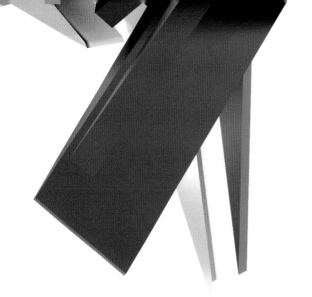

6

METALHEART IS MORE

The DVD-Rom attached to the back side of this book contains a wide variety of digital art files for your perusal – professionally or inspirationally.

1. Royaltyfree media to be used professionally includes: 3D typefaces, 3D objects, backgrounds, seamless tiles, textures, and animated sequences.

2. Animations and video clips from some of our contributing artists, to be enjoyed for inspiration only.

EMBOX METAL TYPE: 3D Typefaces (including alpha channels)

abcdefghijklmnopqrstuvwxyz

ABCDEFGHIJKLMNOPQRSTUVWXYZ

EMBOX NEW METAL PIPE by Anders F Rönnblom. Based on Brainreactor font 'Octane Regular' by Andreas Lindholm.

ABCDEFGHIJKLMNOPQRSTUVWXYZ

EMBOX NEW METAL FAITH by Anders F Rönnblom. Based on Brainreactor font 'Industrial Faith' by Andreas Lindholm.

ABCDEFGHIJKLMNOPQRSTUVWXYZ

EMBOX NEW METAL SURVIVAL by Anders F Rönnblom. Based on Brainreactor font 'Ultimate Survival' by Andreas Lindholm.

ABCDEFGHIJKLMNOPQRSTUVWXYZ

EMBOX NEW METAL RIBBON by Anders F Rönnblom. Based on Brainreactor font 'Intergalactic Veloudrome' by Andreas Lindholm.

ABCDEFGHIJKLMNOPQRSTUVWXYZ

EMBOX NEW METAL MONDO by Anders F Rönnblom. Based on Brainreactor font 'Rip Off Style' by Andreas Lindholm.

abcdefghijklmnopqrstuvwxy

EMBOX NEW METAL MOONSTRING by Anders F Rönnblom. Based on Brainreactor font 'Pornomania' by Andreas Lindholm.

The EMBOX METAL TYPE libraries of 3D typefaces, dingbats and other graphic elements, are produced by Studio Matchbox, Stockholm, Sweden, using RenderMan technology.
Order your customized one-of-a-kind 3D Techno Typeface, single characters or full alphabet sets, for special design projects. For more information: www.macartdesign.matchbox.se

Metalheart Dingbats (including alpha channels)

DINGBAT_01.psd DINGBAT_02.psd DINGBAT_03.psd DINGBAT_04.psd DINGBAT_05.psd DINGBAT_06.psd DINGBAT_07.psd DINGBAT_08.psd

DINGSTAR_01.psd DINGSTAR_02.psd DINGSTAR_03.psd DINGSTAR_04.psd DINGSTAR_05.psd DINGSTAR_06.psd DINGSTAR_07.psd DINGSTAR_08.psd

DINGSTAR_09.psd DINGSTAR_10.psd DINGSTAR_11.psd DINGSTAR_12.psd DINGSTAR_13.psd DINGSTAR_14.psd DINGSTAR_15.psd DINGSTAR_16.psd

Metalheart 2
Metalheart is Movement

CHAPTER 6 (SIX)
Metalheart is More
The DVD

Page 154 - 155

3D Objects (including alpha channels)

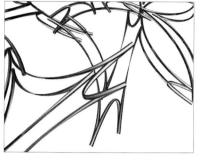

KITSCH_Object01.psd

KITSCH_Object02.psd

KITSCH_Object03.psd

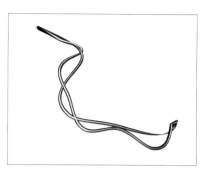

KITSCH_Object04.psd

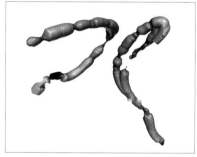

INTERBRAIN_Object01.psd

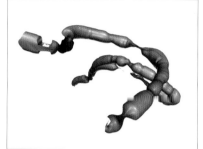

INTERBRAIN_Object02.psd

INTERBRAIN_Object03.psd

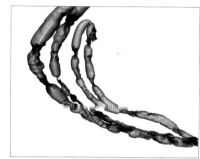

INTERBRAIN_Object04.psd

The Metalheart 3D Objects can be found on CD-Rom Metalheart Vol. 7 and Vol. 8, royaltyfree digital images and graphic elements, published by Agosto Inc. (www.agosto.com).

Metalheart Big Image Background files

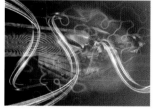

BACKGROUND_01.jpg

BACKGROUND_02.jpg

BACKGROUND_03.jpg

BACKGROUND_04.jpg

BACKGROUND_09.jpg

BACKGROUND_05.jpg

BACKGROUND_06.jpg

BACKGROUND_07.jpg

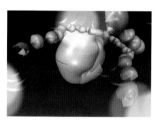

BACKGROUND_08.jpg

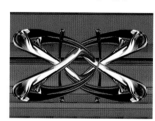

BACKGROUND_10.jpg

The Metalheart Backgrounds, published by Agosto Inc. (www.agosto.com), are royaltyfree digital art images of a high quality. Each 300 dpi image has an approximate file size of 70Mb in RGB mode (93Mb in CMYK).

Metalheart Seamless Tiles

KITSCH_Tile01.jpg

KITSCH_Tile02.jpg

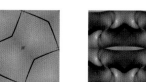

KITSCH_Tile03.jpg

KITSCH_Tile04.jpg

KITSCH_Tile05.jpg

KITSCH_Tile06.jpg

1250_Tile01.jpg

1250_Tile02.jpg

INTERBRAIN_Tile01.jpg   INTERBRAIN_Tile02.jpg   INTERBRAIN_Tile03.jpg   INTERBRAIN_Tile04.jpg   INTERBRAIN_Tile05.jpg   INTERBRAIN_Tile06.jpg   1250_Tile03.jpg   1250_Tile04.jpg

Metalheart Super Tiles (3260 x 102 pixels)

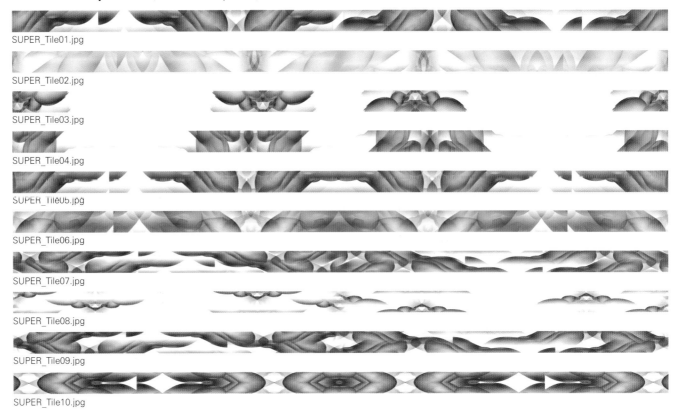

SUPER_Tile01.jpg

SUPER_Tile02.jpg

SUPER_Tile03.jpg

SUPER_Tile04.jpg

SUPER_Tile05.jpg

SUPER_Tile06.jpg

SUPER_Tile07.jpg

SUPER_Tile08.jpg

SUPER_Tile09.jpg

SUPER_Tile10.jpg

Metalheart Gradients

1024x717_Gradient01.jpg

1024x717_Gradient02.jpg

1024x717_Gradient03.jpg

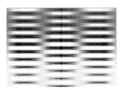

1024x717_Gradient04.jpg

1024x717_Gradient05.jpg

1024x717_Gradient06.jpg

1024x717_Gradient07.jpg

1024x717_Gradient08.jpg

1024x717_Gradient09.jpg

1024x717_Gradient10.jpg

Metalheart Textures

3700x2590_Texture01.jpg

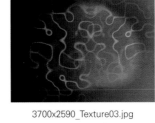

3700x2590_Texture03.jpg

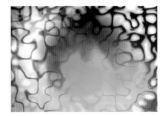

3700x2590_Texture05.jpg

3700x2590_Texture07.jpg

3700x2590_Texture02.jpg

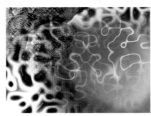

3700x2590_Texture04.jpg

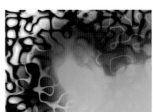

3700x2590_Texture06.jpg

3700x2590_Texture08.jpg

Metalheart 2
Metalheart is Movement

CHAPTER 6 (SIX)
Metalheart is More
The DVD

Page 156 - 157

The Meshmen Textures: Stockholm Subway

Axelsberg04
.jpg

Axelsberg05
.jpg

Axelsberg06
.jpg

Axelsberg08
.jpg

Axelsberg09
.jpg

Axelsberg10
.jpg

Bredang02
.jpg

Bredang03
.jpg

Bredang04
.jpg

Bredang05
.jpg

Bredang07
.jpg

Bredang08
.jpg

Bredang09
.jpg

Fruangen02
.jpg

Fruangen03
.jpg

Fruangen04
.jpg

Fruangen07
.jpg

Fruangen08
.jpg

Fruangen09
.jpg

Fruangen11
.jpg

Fruangen12
.jpg

Fruangen13
.jpg

Fruangen25
.jpg

Hornstull07
.jpg

Hornstull09
.jpg

Hornstull11
.jpg

Hornstull12
.jpg

Hornstull15
.jpg

Liljeholmen02
.jpg

Liljeholmen04
.jpg

Liljeholmen05
.jpg

Liljeholmen09
.jpg

Malarhojden02
.jpg

Malarhojden03
.jpg

Malarhojden05
.jpg

Malarhojden06
.jpg

Malarhojden08
.jpg

Malarhojden09
.jpg

Mariatorget02
.jpg

Mariatorget03
.jpg

Mariatorget04
.jpg

Mariatorget05
.jpg

Mariatorget06
.jpg

Ornsberg02
.jpg

Ornsberg03
.jpg

Ornsberg16
.jpg

Ornsberg17
.jpg

Satra03
.jpg

Satra04
.jpg

Satra05
.jpg

Satra06
.jpg

Satra07
.jpg

Satra08
.jpg

Satra10
.jpg

Satra11
.jpg

Satra12
.jpg

Satra13
.jpg

Satra14
.jpg

Satra17
.jpg

Slussen02
.jpg

Slussen04
.jpg

Slussen05
.jpg

Slussen07
.jpg

Slussen08
.jpg

Slussen10
.jpg

Slussen11
.jpg

Slussen13
.jpg

Slussen14
.jpg

Slussen16
.jpg

Slussen17
.jpg

Slussen18
.jpg

Tcentralen06
.jpg

Tcentralen07
.jpg

Tcentralen08
.jpg

Tcentralen11
.jpg

Tcentralen12
.jpg

Tcentralen13
.jpg

Tcentralen14
.jpg

Tcentralen15
.jpg

Tcentralen16
.jpg

Tcentralen17
.jpg

Tcentralen18
.jpg

Tcentralen19
.jpg

Tcentralen20
.jpg

Tcentralen22
.jpg

Tcentralen23
.jpg

Tcentralen24
.jpg

Vastertorp04
.jpg

Vastertorp05
.jpg

Vastertorp13
.jpg

Vastertorp15
.jpg

Vastertorp16
.jpg

Vastertorp19
.jpg

Zinkensdamm01
.jpg

Zinkensdamm02
.jpg

Zinkensdamm03
.jpg

Zinkensdamm05
.jpg

Zinkensdamm07
.jpg

Zinkensdamm10
.jpg

Guest Artists' Video Clips

PULPVJ by Hinge Design

320 PLASMA by Hinge Design

320 Intro by Hinge Design

HINGE DESIGN is a graphic design and animation studio from New Zealand, working with flyers and record covers and video live art performances.
Name: Robert Zohrab
City/Country: Auckland, New Zealand
E-mail: cybcult@ihug.co.nz
URL: www.cyberculture.co.nz

METAL 1 by Lou Zadesky

METAL 2 by Lou Zadesky

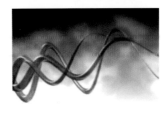

METAL 3 by Lou Zadesky

SCREAMING CACTUS is a design studio in San Francisco, California, run by Lou Zadesky. He specializes in print and web-related design using a variety of 2D and 3D programs, such as Photoshop, 3D Studio Max and After Effects.
Name: Lou Zadesky
City/Country: San Francisco, California, USA
E-mail: lou@screamingcactus.com
URL: www.screamincactus.com

M1NDR3FILL by Suk & Koch

REPLICA by Suk & Koch

SUK & KOCH Media Inc. is a New York-based motion graphics studio working with experimental art and music videos.
E-mail: sk@sukkoch.com
URL: www.sukkoch.com

CYBAJAZ by D-FUSE

SQUAREPUSHER by D-FUSE

D-FUSE work equally in print and web design, they direct and produce music videos, and they create audio/visual installations and experiment with digital filmmaking.
Name: Mike Faukner
City/Country: London, United Kingdom
E-mail: mike@dfuse.com
URL: www.dfuse.com

DUX by Mattias Lindberg

PROZAC NATION by Halvor Bodin

MATTIAS LINDBERG is a Graphic Designer/Animator from Stockholm, Sweden.
E-Mail: mattias@fakepilot.com
URL: www.fakepilot.com

HALVOR BODIN is a graphic designer from Oslo, Norway, who has produced Titles for the feature film PROZAC NATION.
E-Mail: hal@superlow.com
URL: www.superlow.com   www.virtualgarden.no

Join the Metalheart Community

There are three ways you can join the Metalheart Community:
1. REGISTER for the Metalheart Newsletter.
2. SUBMIT your artworks, still images, videos or animations, to the DIGITAL HALL OF FAME AWARD: Metalheart Category.
3. SUBSCRIBE to EFX Art & Design magazine and read the Metalheart Report with the Metalheart Tutorials.
For more information: Please visit www.macartdesign.matchbox.se

Metalheart 2
Metalheart is Movement

CHAPTER 6 (SIX)
Metalheart is More
The DVD
CREDITS

Page 158 - 159